Praise for David

David Winters is a brilliant young literary critic. His literary essays, which have appeared in a vast range of publications, both on- and offline, go far beyond the usual précis-and-evaluation typical of book reviews. He is unique in the philosophical subtlety and depth he brings to his work, and in the striking authors he covers.
Lars Iyer, author of *Spurious*, *Dogma*, and *Exodus*

David Winters is an exceptional talent in literary criticism. He combines a vivid, accessible style of writing with deep erudition and great intellectual precision. Ranging from popular works of fiction to difficult philosophers, he is always able to cut through the jargon and make the reader engage with the heart of the matter. Indeed, Winters is that rare thing: a young intellectual who is able to speak to the general reader while contributing to the academic conversation as well.
Martin Hägglund, Yale University

David Winters is the smartest young critic to emerge in recent years. His writing is marked by a desire for the unorthodox, and an attention to our most daring logophiles – Lish, Lutz, Marcom, Schutt – so often overlooked by others. An intimacy with continental philosophy and literary modernism elevates his work well beyond the obvious exegetical formulas of mainstream criticism, and yet it always remains eminently readable and accessible, eminently fun. In Winters I've found a critic whose writing I can read without having to chalk it up to a guilty pleasure – he makes me smarter, there's no doubt about it.
Evan Lavender-Smith, author of *Avatar* and *From Old Notebooks*

David Winters is a massively intelligent, erudite and inquiring analyst of American letters. I read his essays avidly, and always find fresh insights and fresh connections. He's describing the furniture in the room – a lot of other critics haven't found the door yet. Winters writes with élan, complexity and thoughtfulness. I haven't come across

another new critic I like so well.
Douglas Glover, author of *Attack of the Copula Spiders*

David Winters has become a prominent figure in a new generation of young intellectuals. His literary criticism resists the temptation of liberal humanism and its narrow conception of literature; it interrogates the nature of the novel in a philosophically radical fashion, and sheds light on the alternative voices that are routinely ignored by the mainstream.
Carl Cederström, co-author of *Dead Man Working*

David Winters' meditations on the literary experience dance with intelligence and beauty. Powerful and penetrating, his essays turn other writers' writing into new, exciting pieces that spark the writerly imagination and leave you wanting more. A leading critic.
Susana Medina, author of *Philosophical Toys*

David Winters is the most exciting critic out there. Each of his reviews starts from scratch, as he looks for a new vocabulary and a new form to talk about each new book. In a sense, his reviews are often even more fascinating than the books themselves – demonstrating how great a writer he truly is.
Andrew Gallix, *3:AM Magazine*

Infinite Fictions

Essays on Literature
and Theory

Infinite Fictions

Essays on Literature and Theory

David Winters

Winchester, UK
Washington, USA

First published by Zero Books, 2015
Zero Books is an imprint of John Hunt Publishing Ltd., Laurel House, Station Approach,
Alresford, Hants, SO24 9JH, UK
office1@jhpbooks.net
www.johnhuntpublishing.com
www.zero-books.net

For distributor details and how to order please visit the 'Ordering' section on our website.

Text copyright: David Winters 2014

ISBN: 978 1 78279 803 3
Library of Congress Control Number: 2014948082

A CIP catalogue record for this book is available from the British Library.

Design: Stuart Davies

Printed and bound by CPI Group (UK) Ltd, Croydon, CR0 4YY

We operate a distinctive and ethical publishing philosophy in all
areas of our business, from our global network of authors to
production and worldwide distribution.

CONTENTS

Introduction

Infinite Fictions

Around the time I began writing book reviews, I read that reviewing was "what lice will do, when they have no more blood to suck." If so, the only blood I've ever tasted is mine. Early on, I already knew that my writing wasn't entirely about the books "under review" so much as my internal "reading experience" – though that term might be misleading. In suggesting that my reviews reflect something of my "self," I'm not about to recount my life story, let alone resort to that fashionable form, the "confessional" essay. On the contrary, literary subjectivity isn't always aligned with autobiography. Right now, I'm writing this in the first person, but I perceive that person as a perfect stranger.

Put simply, I've never known who I am. Nor do I feel securely in sync with the world. I intersect with it at an abnormal angle – my link with life is dislocated. Of course, this condition isn't uncommon. I mention it only to emphasize that an initial *alienation* led me to literature. Part of me is predisposed to treat reading as, to quote Houellebecq, a practice that pushes "against the world, against life." At the same time, I don't see reading as simply a passive escape from reality. As Kafka famously says, books can be "like a key to unknown chambers within the castle of oneself." Reading is really a dual movement: books allow us to withdraw from the world, while bringing us back toward it. In reading we disappear, and yet we resurface.

The first section of this collection includes reviews of a range of recent writers, from Lars Iyer to Lydia Davis; Gerald Murnane to Gabriel Josipovici. Here I'll be clear: by writing about these authors rather than others, I'm not projecting a personal canon. I regard reading as an uncertain experience, and not one that lends itself to a normative stance. As a reviewer, all I can do is try to stay true to the texture of that experience. So, these aren't necessarily the "best" books around; they're simply the ones that satisfied me. Strange as it sounds, each of these books briefly allowed me to subtract myself from reality. In this respect, when writing reviews, I'm less intent on making prescriptions than on exploring the space left by my subtraction.

One of the threads running through the first part of this book concerns the writer, teacher, and editor Gordon Lish. Currently, critics still link Lish's name with a tradition of American literary "minimalism." What's less well-known is Lish's longstanding interest in continental philosophy – an influence which led him to formulate, and to *teach*, certain distinctive ideas about fictive form. I write about Lish's ideas directly in my review of his startling novel, *Peru*. Perhaps more usefully, I also track those ideas' diffusion through the prose styles of Lish's students – including Sam Lipsyte, Sam Michel, Gary Lutz, and Dawn Raffel. In collecting this cluster of pieces, my hope is that I'll help a handful of readers to reassess an overlooked aspect of American letters.

When I last spoke with Lish, he described fiction as a "bounded infinity" – an object which seems circumscribed on all sides, but which contains a limitless internal world. For Lish, literary form is a bit like the physics of turbulence; it's all about how nonlinear patterns produce emergent effects. In their different ways, he and his students create self-sufficient totalities, by manipulating the smallest linguistic units. As Lish says of Diane Williams – a writer I lack the skill to review – "it is the genius of this artist to make her bondage a fabulous abode," in which "all the rooms she cannot escape" are magically "made lavish." More broadly, though, this is but one perspective on what might be called fiction's inner "infinitude." There are countless others, and one of the purposes of this book is to begin to build a picture of them.

I've described my experience of reading as an immersion in a peculiar kind of fictional space. Above all, what fascinates me about that space is the idea that it might be infinite; that the world opened up by a book might exceed that outside it. I get glimpses of this infinity in the linguistic fractals fashioned by Lish's brilliant student, Jason Schwartz. But I also see it in the South African author Ivan Vladislavić, who has written a Borgesian fable about an unlimited library of unwritten books. I see it, too, in the horizonless "brightly lit background" depicted by the Australian genius Gerald Murnane; in the expansive skies evoked by the American pastoralist Dylan Nice; and in the mythical underworld mapped by Miranda Mellis. Reading these writers, I start to sense that there's something alive in the background of writing; some inexhaustible source of light and silence.

Are "infinite" fictions simply whirlpools in which one loses oneself, or might they furnish forms of self-reflection? Describing the task of autobiography, Frank Kermode remarks that recollection isn't really a question of facts, but of "the weather, the private weather, unpredictable as dreams, yet recognizable as a climate." Similarly, even a trivial book review – and triviality is among the allures of the form – can be a barometer of its writer's private weather. Whatever we write, we reveal more than we mean to; as Kristeva says, "the speaking subject gives herself away." I wouldn't say I give much away in my writing, but some of it still speaks obliquely of secret experiences: depression, religion, unrequited love. Try as I might, I can't write about books like Stasiuk's *Dukla*, or Nice's *Other Kinds*, without tacitly taking my existential temperature. Such "weather patterns" aren't made explicit in these pieces, yet they exist in their atmosphere.

In a way, to write a review is to hide behind what another, better writer has written. Literary criticism has been described as "thinking with an object," but thinking always transforms its objects into other things. In the course of a review, a book can become a crutch, a mirror, a mask. In my case, the deictic aspect of reviewing – its "aboutness" – lets me pretend that my words refer *only* to my object, and not to myself. Sometimes, while writing, I briefly believe that I'm not *revealed* by my speech – that I can't be caught or found out. That doesn't last, and, looking back, I'm made aware of the ways I'm laid bare. For instance, I've observed that my reviews often concern fiction's internal worlds, and their capacity to counterbalance the real one. Already though, I recognize that this is less a respectable intellectual interest, more an expression of a personal need for refuge. I've tried to rationalize my critical practice, but finally it's about something basic and frail: art as solace.

The second section of this book is called "On Theory," and it contains reviews of various works of criticism and philosophy. These pieces aim to present accessible sketches of critical concepts like deconstruction, "distant reading," trauma theory, and modernism (among others). Along the way, they also attend to overarching questions about theory's intellectual history. This history can be seen from the standpoint of a kind of symptomatic psychology (as in Peter Sloterdijk's "portrait of the theorist as a young man") or in terms of institutional sociology (as in Martin Woessner's reception history of Heidegger's writings). Complementarily, the history of theory can also be understood by studying the internal logic of theoretical *concepts* – an approach I explore in my reviews of D.N. Rodowick and Tom Eyers, for example.

If my taste in fiction is shaped by my lived experience, can the same be said of my fascination with theory? Clearly, the very idea of theory implies a distinction from everyday life. But, as Sloterdijk shows (a little like Nietzsche does, or Bourdieu), theory's supposed autonomy is largely illusory. In his classic work *Keywords*, Raymond Williams defines "theory" as "a scheme of ideas which explains practice." However, he also cites a seventeenth-century source, which diagnoses "theory and contemplation" as "nothing but waking men's dreams, and sick men's phantasies." This latter aspect comes closer to what interests me. Dreams don't come from nowhere, and neither do theories; both are produced by processes of condensation and displacement. Ultimately, theory is not isolable from life. Instead, it's more like an *image* of life, in all its sickness and inexplicability. Consequently, to ask the question "what is theory?" is also always to ask, "what does theory mean to me?"

A lot of us know what it's like to have *learned* about theory, but what is it like to have *lived* it? Writing about students' early exposure to theory, François Cusset coins the term *Bildungstheorie* – a word which cleverly captures the "mechanism of enchantment" whereby "certain students, particularly those alienated from societal norms," are "inspired by a word, a motif, or a thematic tendency," to the extent that it alters their "existential landscape." Crucially, claims Cusset, this kind of primal encounter comes *prior* to proper comprehension. Initially, theory conveys not information but inspiration – before it is thought, it is felt. Whether we read Adorno or Agamben, Barthes or Benjamin, our reading begins in an emotive engagement with unknown words, charismatic codes, and foreign tongues. Not knowing, but *feeling* our way around theory, we acquire an affective investment in its ideas. This is the psychic life of theory – the level at which it is less a technical instrument than a totem or talisman; a charm that we clasp to our hearts.

Maybe the same sort of life lives in reading itself. Renata Adler remarks of her reading that "some of the things that had meant the most to me, I had completely misunderstood." Elizabeth Hardwick claims that "in reading, I enter a sort of hallucinatory state." Eve Sedgwick evokes the "speculative, superstitious" reading practices of young children, for whom understanding "seeps in only from the most stretched and ragged edges of competence." Reading is not the same thing as knowing. Nor, for that matter, is reviewing. I've already mentioned the triviality of the form, and I'm aware of the vanity of assembling this kind of collection. I wouldn't want to present these pieces of writing as anything more than what they are: the scattered, erratic traces of one reader's life. Nor do they even reflect a directed *program* of reading. Really, they're only records of my desperate autodidacticism. The autodidact, observes Bourdieu, can't help but "betray the arbitrariness of his knowledge" – the chaotic quality of a learning guided by "biographical accidents." For me, reviewing, like reading, is inseparably linked to this living chaos. So, to conclude, I'll echo Bourdieu. In the end, if these pieces add up to anything, hopefully it's enough that they add up to this: "a collection of unstrung pearls, accumulated in the course of an uncharted exploration."

On Literature

Language as Astonishment

Micheline Aharonian Marcom, *A Brief History of Yes*

Writing about the work of Micheline Aharonian Marcom is likely to leave one searching for words. Each of her books has been newly, bravely bewildering, in ways that are almost beyond paraphrase. That is, these texts assert such stylistic strength that they seem to resist the language of criticism, or any language other than their own. How can prose so poetically self-reliant, so set apart from our "ordinary" discourse, be faithfully described, let alone criticized, from outside? Confronted with this kind of writing, any critical review – any act of writing *about* – could run the risk of redundancy.

In fact, if words must be ventured about Marcom, "risk" is perhaps an appropriate one to open with. Most noticeably, she has taken risks with her subject matter. Her first three novels, *Three Apples Fell from Heaven*, *The Daydreaming Boy*, and *Draining the Sea* addressed the traumatic aftermath of genocide in Armenia and Guatemala. This trilogy told graphic stories of torture and brutality, but in an intensely poetic diction – a feat few writers might have attempted, for fear of merely aestheticizing atrocity. Her fourth book, *The Mirror in the Well*, explored a contrasting extreme of experience: eroticism, and specifically female sexuality, rendered with a rare explicitness – a fierce physicality far beyond that of Nin, or Lawrence, or other familiar landmarks of the genre.

Marcom's new novel, *A Brief History of Yes*, is less overtly transgressive than its predecessor – less centered on sex than on solitude; on the loneliness left after love is over. Previously, Marcom scaled the peak of what two people can do together, whereas now she digs into what drives them apart. So if *Mirror* expressed ecstasy, *Yes* explores ecstasy's ebbing. In this sense the texts are twinned, like the rise and fall of a single cycle. Both books concentrate closely on a couple; a woman and a man. In both, the narration is weighted towards, or focalized through, the woman's emotions and sensations. And each of these couples acquires an almost archetypal quality. *Mirror* made a point of anonymity: in homage to Marguerite Duras, it gave us no names, only "girl" and "boy," "lover" and "beloved." *Yes* treats these terms like traces of memory – each occurs only occasionally, but continues to echo over the text. Although Marcom now names her protagonist, her writing still ripples with namelessness, as if recalling a commonality that has been lost.

Of course, loss is the very locus of this novel. Marcom is not preoccupied with plot; her writing reads more like an open inquiry into her chosen emotion. Essentially, the novel contains only one concretely plotted "event" – a Portuguese woman, Maria, is suddenly left by her lover, an unnamed American man. Moreover, this dissolution doesn't occur at the crux of a narrative arc, but at the book's outset: for both Maria and the reader, the love affair is always and already over, "its end entailed at its inception." Hence narrative convention is overturned by something closer to the lived experience of loss: rather like in life, a relationship's end retrospectively alters its memory.

In this respect, as always in Marcom, the object of writing informs its form. Here, heartbreak requires not linear description, but circular distillation – a technique of "telling it over and over again," to cite Gertrude Stein. This circularity also aligns with the book's symbolism: the liaison lasts "a calendar year, August to August," closing up on itself at its end. But love's underlying recursive rhythm – the sense in which its loss *completes* it – is played out more subtly through Marcom's poetic style, which repeats and reprises the same small set of remembered circumstances. The resulting text is not so much a "novel," more an attempt to render the structure of sorrowful memory.

For when we look back at our losses, as Marcom writes, our minds rarely stick to a "story." Rather, we accumulate an "augmenting account," in which "only the weight of increase remains," the wash of color that overcomes our memories as they fade.

The text therefore tracks the everyday alchemy – the act of internal *translation* – through which facts transform into memories, and memories merge into emotions. Marcom knows that there are no words for this process; that language can't capture a lost lover's afterlife in the mind. But what can't be articulated can still be obliquely attested to. Marcom marks her impossible object by means of the word *saudade* – a Portuguese term picked partly because of its lack of a direct English equivalent. Maria ruminates on its meaning, describing it as "the love that remains after the beloved has gone." This formulation suggests a significant ambiguity. In *saudade*, the negative path of nostalgia produces a positive outcome: love may be gone, but as long as its memory remains, love returns to itself; it goes on. This is why Maria says of her sadness that "I love this feeling as I love love… this after-love feeling." And this is also the sense in which, in the end, she says *yes* – to death, which clears the ground for "growth," to absence, "another form of presence," and to grief, which is "not ground but sky… so she is uplifted."

Marcom has remarked that her book was inspired by *fado* – the genre of Portuguese song that stages the sadness of *saudade*. But *fado* is only a formal precedent insofar as it sings the unsayable. The truth is that this book disrupts any generic method, just as it disrupts received rules of grammar and syntax. To this extent, its style exhibits what the critic Derek Attridge has called "singularity" – where singular works are those "that surprise, that disturb, that find new modes of representation and new objects to represent." This quality is evident everywhere in *Yes*, but it is worth picking a typical passage:

Water. The water in the glass. The clear glass, the clear water. Water and the glass the same color which is clear and the word clear which doesn't say the yes of the color or the isness of all of life in the color or nothing in the glass holding water oxygen light refracted on the glass which is the image on glass of the window, the blue peeking sky, fingerprints, greasy and earthy, so that the glass doesn't fly off into ethereal metaphors and the girl herself, Maria, in the glass: thin stretched-down face, dark eyes, the right darker than the left, the right hand lifted in prayer, in benediction, and the mouth smiling now, open, saying, singing herself.

Here the word "water" spills out a stream of language that liquidates language. Marcom mounts a metalinguistic attack on linguistic mechanics – note the embedded critique of the word "clear," and the stated resistance to "metaphors." These are the poles she steers between, like Scylla and Charybdis. The less clear her prose grows, the more oceanic, eliminating the edges between objects. There ensues a direct, non-metaphorical amalgamation of water, glass, window, and sky. Not only this, but the newly blurred sensory manifold is itself blurred with the consciousness that observes it: Maria's reflection makes her *continuous* with the water. Such is the song that many of Marcom's best sentences sing – proceeding by association and intuition, led less by rules than by faith, and always leading somewhere unforeseen: language as astonishment. No longer a bridge from A to B, writing is the water that rages beneath. Later on in *Yes*, a character talks of the "delicate wildness" of nature. The words might apply just as well to this writing; to the delicate wildness of its singular style.

If Marcom allows wildness to arise within language, this returns us to the question of risk. The risks writers take can be construed in crude terms – say, as a lack of concession to the "common reader," or a courting of controversial content. But

Marcom's writing is also attuned to the subtler risks of style – or rather, it radically recasts style *as* risk. One of the lessons of her work is that fidelity to experience necessarily deforms familiar language. And if pursued with *sufficient* fidelity, this deformation will put the whole work at risk. To write in a truly unprecedented style is to ensure that the work stands or falls on that style. To be sure, Marcom's work doesn't always succeed – but its failures remain far richer, stronger, and more singular than those of works that fear imperfection.

In this respect, her writing takes risks not to secure "success," but to effect an *experience* of exigency and exhilaration. Rilke once wrote that works of art can only be judged on whether they have "arisen out of necessity." In Marcom, style is the sign of that necessity; of an artwork's urgent, internal need for its object to speak its *own* language, and no other. More recently than Rilke, Susan Sontag spoke of this trait in terms of stylistic "inevitability." The strongest works, Sontag argued, are those "so wholly centered in their style" that they "seem secreted, not constructed." The phrase rings equally true here too. To read Marcom, then, is to read writing that risks being the sole instance of its species – words that could *only* have been written the way they are written.

Work the Hurt

Sam Lipsyte, *The Fun Parts*

In an article about the stories his sportswriter father told him as a child, Sam Lipsyte remembers a revelation which "cracked the world right open for me." Always a "nervous" boy, Sam wondered whether stars like Howard Cosell and Muhammad Ali were "nice" to his dad. "What the fuck does it matter," he was quizzed in return, "if everyone is nice or not?" The decisive insight was that it didn't; that only "the story mattered, and a story with everybody being nice wasn't much of a story anyway."

The thirteen stories in *The Fun Parts* impart similarly sharp lessons. Lipsyte's latest book, after novels *Home Land* and *The Ask*, marks a return to the short form in which he began, recalling the already classic *Venus Drive*. And like that collection, *The Fun Parts* showcases stories whose sheer telling – their force; their rhythmic momentum – tends to matter more than what they tell of. So if there is no "niceness" to be found in *The Fun Parts* (a book every bit as abrasive as *The Ask*) this could be because, stylistically, storytelling calls more clearly for cruelty. Lipsyte's luckless characters can be read as casualties of his craft; their misfortunes are functions of his stories' composition – and are all the funnier for it.

Lipsyte's stylistic tactics, learned partly from his teacher Gordon Lish, involve what the latter refers to as "torque," "swerve," and "refactoring." Although these terms sound opaque, the point they're meant to make is specific. For Lish, and similarly for Lipsyte, a successful story is one which relentlessly ratchets up its internal pressure, partly by feeding its linguistic output back into its input – like a nonlinear system in physics, or feedback on a guitar amp. Such a story starts with a sentence setting an initial condition. The second sentence reconfigures the first, curving or swerving back into it. The next sentence swerves harder still, and so on, always with the aim of raising the stakes, tightening the tautness. For instance, in a typical sequence from *The Fun Parts*, a story's narrator says of his father:

> You had to hand it to him. I generally want to hand it to him, and then, while he's absorbed in admiring whatever I've handed to him, kick away at his balls. That's my basic strategy. Except he has no balls. Testicular cancer.

What makes this paragraph's punchline comedic is that it's utterly unpredictable. And it's unpredictable because it is produced not by a premeditated plot, but by something almost like an algorithm. Here as elsewhere, Lipsyte's writing runs not from A to B to C, but from A^1 to A^2 to A^3, each sentence increasing the energy in the system, bringing it to a boil, and hence setting off unexpected explosions.

Another example: in the story "The Real-Ass Jumbo," a character contemplates the future. Next thing we know, we see "his sister gang-raped in an abandoned Target outside Indianapolis." But before our brains can process this information, we learn that "strangest of all, he didn't have a sister," a surprise which in turn adds "urgency to his vision." Indeed, it is Lipsyte's spiraling search for urgency that creates these chaotic outcomes – in this he is a writer for whom, as Lish once put it, "the job is not to know what you are going to find." So if a character contracts cancer, or is created solely to be assaulted in a discount store, it's because that's what Lipsyte's escalatory logic entails.

Hard luck for them, but what makes this method compelling is that, like the blind fate that the Greeks called *heimarmene*, it closely reflects the cruel yet comic complexity of real life. About this, *The Fun Parts* is emphatic: "the world is not a decent place to live," decides one narrator. Another notes that life is like "a fish tank nobody cleans: just fish shit and dead fish." Stories like

"Snacks" and "The Dungeon Master" dwell on the agonies of adolescence, charting the loss of a childhood in which "the world still seemed like something that could save me from the hurt, not be it."

But the world is the hurt in these stories – the void they reveal so remorselessly. In this respect, writing should "work the hurt," as a charlatan child-minder urges a breastfeeding mother in one of the book's more boisterous moments. Life is bitter; it will "bite your eyes out," but Lipsyte knows better than to express the pain of existence directly, unswervingly. "You can't share pain," a holocaust survivor reminds a recovering drug addict in "Deniers." So, to work the hurt isn't simply to share it but rather to see it and raise it, refactoring it through a story's style as much as its substance.

In "Nate's Pain is Now," the standout story of *The Fun Parts*, a writer of misery memoirs hears to his horror (and our humor) that his hurt has been trumped by that of a rival martyr. Demoralized, he goes for a walk by the river, where his ruminations give rise to a riff which is worth quoting at length:

> I hated them, the gays, the straights. The races. The genders and ages. None of them loved me. I was feeling that forlorn hum. Maybe another memoir was burbling up.
>
> Home, I called Jenkins, my agent.
>
> "Nate stole my style," I told him. "My wife."
>
> "Your agent, too," said Jenkins.
>
> "I feel that forlorn hum coming on," I said. "It's going to be the best book yet. I've really suffered this time."
>
> "It's over."
>
> "What do you mean it's over?"
>
> "It's Nate's time."

This sketch displays several distinctive Lipsytian tricks, from his trademark telegraphic compression ("home," not "when I got home") to the ironic elision of narrative voice and natural dialogue. For instance, the phrase "forlorn hum" first occurs in the narrative, where we're predisposed to permit its literary diction. But by later rerouting it into reported speech, Lipsyte renders it ridiculous, undermining his narrator's state of mind by means of mere repetition. Incidentally, this very device is reversed in "Deniers," where a piece of clichéd speech – "people ought to keep their traps shut" – returns in a defamiliarized form in the next sentence of narrative: "American traps tended to hang open." In this way, the everyday is replayed as rhythmic poetry.

From its opening salvos, the section above seems intent on intensification – inflating from "gays" to "straights" to everyone, ever; from "style" to "wife" to a lifetime now over. But what's being built up is also breaking down. By the end the narrator is left with nothing; even his forlornness has lost all foundation. In this, Lipsyte's prose is like a ladder, but it's one he constructs as he climbs, at each step removing the rung below and placing it overhead. He works the hurt by heightening it with one hand, while undercutting it with the other. This is why we get vertigo when Lipsyte launches one-liners like "I'd found my calling, even when the calls never came." It's also why reading these stories means meeting them in the making – witnessing writing being brought to birth in the midst of its disappearance. And beneath all of this, we glimpse the abyss: Lipsyte's ladder is always poised over a void, whether it takes the shape of Nate's pain, an old man's exposed cock in "The Climber Room," or indeed a demonic, devouring mouth at the end of "The Real-Ass Jumbo."

Some might see this as a sign that Lipsyte puts style over substance, but that would be missing the point. He's best understood as a satirist, and satire uses style to reveal the substance reality lacks. Still, it's true that his high-wire techniques seem more suited to short fiction than to full-length novels. This is of course a shortcoming he shares with several other students of Lish. The trouble is that his style is so strong as to leave little room for novelistic polyphony – the perspectival variation of voices that critic Mikhail Bakhtin posits as the key to the genre. Even when Lipsyte would like to try multiple viewpoints – as in "The Republic of Empathy," which features four human narrators, not to mention an artificially intelligent Reaper drone – individual idiolects are soon subsumed in a single Lipsytian voice. His style simply can't stay away from the spotlight; as soon as it takes to the stage it's the star performer, the story's overriding imperative.

Yet this, in fact, is part of the fun of *The Fun Parts*. It's fine to call Lipsyte's fictions "stories," but let's not be led too far astray by such shorthand. These pieces of prose aren't primarily narratives – not expositions of events; still less parables or exempla – so much as stylistic machines, whose sole purpose is to stay in motion. Or rather, for Lipsyte a well-wrought story is like an athletic performance: a single, continuous gesture, akin to kicking a ball or, to evoke "Ode to Oldcorn," putting a shot. In that latter tale, Lipsyte lingers on a recollection of what a shot looks like when airborne, released with the optimum "Oldcorn torque, Oldcorn spin." As the narrator remembers, "I could almost see it fly off his fingertips, hang there in the day skies of my mind, an iron moon." And this is the state a story should reach: that miraculous moment when a shot stays aloft on its own; or when an arrow appears to propel itself once the bowstring is pulled and let go.

In consequence, where traditional stories tend towards closure, Lipsyte's seem to reach for ecstatic release. A case in point is "Deniers," whose main character, Mandy, is an ex-junky in search of "closure" of her own. Here, however, is where she winds up in the freewheeling final paragraph:

Tomorrow... she'd begin her project of helping everybody she could help, and after that she'd head out on a great long journey to absolutely nowhere and write a majestic poem cycle steeped in heavenly lavender-scented closure and also utter despair, a poem cycle you could also actually ride for its aerobic benefits, and she'd pedal that fucker straight across the face of the earth until at some point she'd coast right off the edge, whereupon she'd giggle and say, "Oh, shit."

Only the keenest of readers will recognize Lipsyte's skill in swerving his story to such a climax. Yes, it's cartoonishly funny, and "fun is important," as we're reminded elsewhere in the book. But its funniness also forms part of a masterful formal maneuver. Here, spun and thrown, a story has reached a speed where style and substance become one – so that when it's cut short at its summit it seems to describe itself, measuring its own motion. Moreover, maybe American writing has always been motivated by such motion: remember Walt Whitman's poetic spider, working above an abyss, historyless, spinning "filament, filament, filament, out of itself; ever unreeling them – ever tirelessly speeding them." Almost like spider webs, when looked at closely, Lipsyte's stories exhibit a near-geometrical elegance. They're fun; they hurt; they have fun with hurt; but under it all is the sound of silk spinning and quickening, arcing from nothing to nothing – or the sight of an iron moon in mid-flight.

Like Sugar Dissolving

Lydia Davis, *The End of the Story*

Lydia Davis's fiction is not only, as nearly everyone notes, difficult to categorize; it is also surprisingly difficult to comprehend. Surprising, that is, insofar as the seeming simplicity of Davis's style is simple only at first sight, while the humdrum familiarity of her subject matter conceals, under a placid surface, a dizzying capacity for defamiliarization. And in making us dizzy, Davis also attunes us to a distinctive blend of literature and philosophy. Her familiarity with the thought of Blanchot, Leiris, and the like is well-known. However, such influences aren't crudely restricted to the "content" of her stories – after all, fictions which flashily *allude* to philosophy arguably only fetishize it, as a sort of accessory. Instead, Davis incorporates philosophy into the fine grain of her writing. Her fiction's philosophical force manifests in the fidelity of its linguistic form to the treacherous texture of everyday experience. Hence, if it is hard to get a purchase on Davis's prose, that might be precisely the point. As the critic and psychoanalyst Josh Cohen puts it in his essay "Reflexive Incomprehension,"

> Davis's minimal style, with its studied casualness of tone, the very American ordinariness of its idiom, has the paradoxical effect of inducing us to listen to an anterior dimension of language. This style is mimed in her fiction's microscopically exacting focus on the contingent detail of everyday life, bringing to light a stubbornly untranslatable enigma at the heart of the ordinary. Davis estranges language not by setting it apart from everyday speech but by putting us in an almost uncomfortable proximity to it, forcing us to hear resonances of the unknown in the most familiar.

If the direction of Davis's writing tends toward, as she once observed in an interview, "philosophical investigation," perhaps it is fitting that almost all of it falls into the category of the short story – a form which, in her hands, affirms its affinities with the *pensée*, the fragment, the meditation. For this reason, it is tempting to treat her only novel (and this in a career of over thirty years) as an anomaly. The fact that this is far from the case confirms not only the consistency of her thematic concerns but also the concentrated quality of her authorial consciousness, which articulates long and short forms alike along comparable lines, always with the same steadfast focus.

The "story" of *The End of the Story* is, as suggested above, deceptively simple. An unnamed narrator (who, like Davis, works as a translator) looks back on a love affair long since over. As with any such loss, she "couldn't let go of it later." So, looking back at herself not letting go, she tries to imprint an order upon her experience. Specifically, she sets out to turn the story of the failed affair and its aftermath into a novel. Already though, this apparently straightforward story is mediated through multiple optics. Firstly, there are the facts; secondly, the narrator's slanted experience of those facts. Next, there are the mechanisms of memory – always frail and fallible – through which this experience is recalled. Finally, framing this nested structure, we confront the encompassing act of writing – an act which, as Blanchot would have it, "issues from its own absence, addressing itself to the shadow of events, not their reality." More confusingly still, if writing is the final stage of this sequence, it is also the first, since writing is what renders recollection. And this is to say nothing of the difference between the novel the narrator is writing and the one we are reading – the one written by Lydia Davis. Writing is a shadow that casts its own shadow.

This might be what Michael Hoffman means when he writes in his review of the novel that the narrative is "distanced or framed or negated" to such a degree that it is bathed in "negative space," evoking an aesthetic of the "visionary negative." The narrator's state after the end of the affair (amplified all the more by the mediations of writing and memory) is one of profound uncertainty. Profound but thoroughly familiar, for we need not have read Descartes to recognize this kind of proliferating doubt:

> I did not have good answers for my questions. I could always find a few answers for each question, but I wasn't satisfied with them: though they seemed to answer the question, the question did not go away. Why had he claimed on the telephone, when I called him long distance, that we were still together and there was nothing to worry about? Was he ever truly tempted to come back to me after I returned? Why did he send me that French poem a year later? Did he ever receive my answer? If he did, why didn't he answer it?

The fretful tenor of such passages – the air of escalating insecurity that Thad Ziolkowski has dubbed "high analytical vertigo" – is almost omnipresent in Davis. And her subject matter is often similarly consistent. In this respect, *The End of the Story* represents the fruition (or the slowly fading afterimage) of a theme begun in Davis's breakthrough collection *Break it Down* – a book which, like this one, fixates on failed romances and their wreckage. Indeed, the collection's opening story, simply titled "Story," contains content which Davis directly incorporates into her novel. In each text, for example, the narrator neurotically ruminates over her (ex-) lover, to the point of spying on him through his window. And in "Story" as in *The End of the Story*, this act of obsessive observation is inspired by a desire to "figure it out," to "come to some conclusions about such questions as: whether he is angry or not; if he is, then how angry… whether he loves me or not; how much; how capable he is of deceiving me," and so on.

"The Letter" (also collected in *Break it Down*) rehearses a similar scene of incertitude, likewise replayed in the novel. Here the former lover sends the narrator a French poem (untitled, although the line *"compagnon de silence"* implies that it is Valéry's *Le bois amical*) from which she then tries to surmise his intentions. In so doing, she subjects the letter's language to a restless speculation remarkably similar to that which mediates memories in *The End of the Story*. For instance, "if there can be no doubt about *retrouvions*," she reflects, then she "can believe that he is still thinking, eight hundred miles from here, that it will still be possible ten years from now, or five years, or, since a year has already passed, nine years or four years from now." Later, while "half dreaming" over the letter, she senses that "something of his smell may still be in the paper," although she is "probably smelling only the ink."

If the recurrence of such scenes suggests certain steady preoccupations in Davis's work during this period, it also points beyond matters of content, toward an ambience or attitude that permeates much of her writing. Whether it is applied to a memory, a word from a poem, or a sensory perception, her narrators' style of analysis is similar: in each case, a hyperconscious observer hopes "to decide what I could be sure of, and what I didn't know." But time and again, the drive to decide only results in further indecision. The struggle to stabilize an object (a poetic line in a foreign language; a silhouette glimpsed through a window) intensifies its instability, leaving it blurred beyond recognition. Borrowing Graham Harman's philosophical terminology, we might observe that such objects "withdraw," exceeding their external relations. In Davis, moreover, the object's recession reveals the rocks on which thought runs aground. That is, the world itself withdraws like a tide, uncovering a widening gap which consciousness unfolds to fill ("ten years from now, or five years, or, since a year has already passed, nine years or four years from now") until it saturates itself, *ad absurdum*.

The severance of subject from object in Davis's work – the way the mind finds itself shipwrecked, in the wake of a withdrawing world – can be characterized, according to Josh Cohen's above-mentioned essay, as a condition of "reflexive incomprehension." Self-reflexive works of fiction – texts in which narrative consciousness fills the frame of reference, twisting and turning in on itself – typically tend, Cohen claims, toward a "subversion of knowledge" which is simultaneously a "recovery." Put simply, literary reflexivity undercuts received "truths" so as to express a deeper truth, at a further turn of the screw. However, Davis's narratives run in a more disconcerting direction. Going against the grain of reflexive revelation, her writing "repeatedly carries us across an elaborate, often labyrinthine logical and emotional pathway only to leave both narrator and reader in ignorance." The mind's modulating inquiries cannot exhaustively capture reality. Instead, every attempt at explanation merely exacerbates the mystery.

This mystery – the residuum that remains when reality is incompletely "broken down" – returns us to the "negative space" that Hoffman discerns in Davis's novel. Cohen describes this enigmatic effect in terms of the Levinasian *il y a* (literally, the "there is"), a stratum of "undetermined, anonymous being" that silently subtends our lived experience. The *il y a* is the neutral, impersonal "background" of existence: what life would look like with the lights out. Davis's style of incomprehension seems closely aligned with such a dimension, perhaps even producing it, as if through a kind of epistemological echo. Her prose's proximity to this unpopulated plane could also account for those commonly occurring passages – such as this, from the story "Therapy" – which strike an almost baffling pitch of banality:

> At first, I would only sit in a chair picking hair and dust off my clothes, and then get up and stretch and sit down again. In the morning I drank coffee and smoked. In the evening I drank tea and smoked and went to the window and back and

from one room into the next room.

The peculiar coloring of such descriptions – minimal, muted, but numinously so, as if touched by the aura of all the events they leave unregistered – resembles the silence that fills the air after the voicing of a question. That such questions remain unanswered reflects Davis's sensitivity to quotidian flatness – her eye for the empty expanses of the everyday – yet it also suggests something more metaphysical. What matters most in Davis is not so much the specific sense of a given question, nor the identity of its addressee (thus, in the novel, the lover is left unnamed) but the fundamental fact that the question "does not go away." Somewhere between the self and the world, Davis's narratives paint the blank canvas of the question's persistence. At this level, a book like *The End of the Story* is less about a love affair than a universal enigma – after all, the narrator's endless questioning could equally well be addressed to an absent God. So the problem is not simply that we cannot recapture our lost loves; rather, it is that reality itself is unresolved and radically answerless.

The End of the Story plays out against such a background of answerlessness, balancing as if above an abyss. The tightrope the narrator walks is tethered to her ideal of "order" – a law which she wants to apply to the "story." Order, however, is hard to establish:

> I need to put more order into what I remember. The order is difficult. It has been the most difficult thing about this book... I have tried to find a good order, but my thoughts are not orderly – one is interrupted by another, or one contradicts another, and in addition to that, my memories are quite often false, confused, abbreviated, or collapsed into one another.

Davis herself has remarked of her novel that "what interested me, in the end, was how the narrator's mind worked, not the actual experience of the love affair." However, her statement belies the extent to which these two terms end up seeming indistinguishable. The narrative's real interest lies in the way the mind occludes and eclipses actual experience – indeed, this is what produces the book's unique pathos. If the narrator is perpetually "in the wrong place to understand, either too far inside each thing or too far outside it," there is something quietly tragic about her awareness that her own mind has caused this confusion. She is, in this sense, inseparable from her sadness, which is instinctive and internal – her heartbreak is part of her, rather than part of the world.

In some respects it is easy to forget – and thus unsettling to recollect – that every event in this book is a mental event; every character a construction of one woman's memory. Of course, her frequent metafictional reflections (where she self-consciously frets over the shape of the story) disrupt our suspension of disbelief, and press against the prospect of order. More importantly, though, they remind us that what we are reading is not the thing itself but the thought; that the book follows the faulty logic of memory formation, leaving its fabric full of rifts and ripples. "I see that I'm shifting the truth around a little," the narrator admits, "at certain points accidentally, but at others deliberately," just as we do when retrospectively reassessing a relationship. And, as always, it is the accidental aspects of memory that prove the most painful – those tiny cracks and inaccuracies that increase the distance between us and what we want to recall. Consider Davis's narrator, reminiscing about the first night she spent with her lover:

By the front wall he lifted a stem of thorns that hung down from an overgrown climbing rose so that I could pass without scratching myself. Or maybe he couldn't have done this in the dark, and it was on another day, in the daylight. Or it was that night, but the night was not entirely dark. In fact, it is only dark in my memory of that particular night, because I know there were two bright streetlamps nearby: one of them shone into my room.

If it is dark in her memory, this may be because memory always darkens its objects, slowly corroding their reality and replacing them with simulacra. Of the lover himself, she notes that she is "used to the version of his face" she has crafted from memory: "if I saw a clear picture of him, I would have to get used to a new face." She is also aware that writing partakes of the same corrosive process as remembering – such that "there were days when I wrote about him so much that he was no longer quite real; I had managed to drain him of his substance, and fill my notebook with it, which would mean that in some sense I had killed him." Hence, the entity to which her writing refers is not the man she once knew; it is only his imprecise mental image. The consequence of this, as Christopher Knight acutely comments in his essay on the novel, is that "the narrator's relation with him increasingly looks like a relation with herself." The sensation is similar to when we see a stranger's face in a crowd, thinking, fleetingly, that it belongs to a friend. Here, however, there is only one face, one consciousness, isolated and delimited.

Accordingly, *The End of the Story* seems to assume the form of a firmly closed circle. The narrative maps the outlines of a mind whose contents, despite their dissimilar surfaces, are crystallized from a single substance. Within the world of this book, the flickering mirages known by names like "lover" and "novel" are only modes of the narrator's aloneness. Moreover, this structure mirrors the fact that we know, from the start, that the romance is over – making its end a prerequisite of its beginning. This colors the narrator's memories of her relationship, imbuing even the earliest moments with an atmosphere of finality:

After he left me, the beginning was not only the first, happy occasion; it also contained the end, as though the very air of that room where we sat together, in that public place, where he leaned over, barely knowing me, and whispered to me, were already permeated with the end of it, as though the walls of that room were already made of the end of it.

Perhaps the remembrance of things past cannot help but be "permeated" with their end. The closure of this cognitive loop is enacted when Davis's novel concludes by returning to its opening scene – in which the narrator sits in a bookstore, whose owner offers her some "bitter tea." This scene, she explains, "ceremonially" marks the "end" of her short-lived relationship; and with it the end of her novelization. Nonetheless, in itself, it is of no obvious purpose. As elsewhere in Davis, the foregrounded moment is merely what Franco Moretti would call a "filler." That is, the scene exemplifies those empty measures that often occur when narrative finds itself idle – sitting; smoking; drinking tea; passing time while awaiting the next event or epiphany. Such insignificant interludes might make up much of a typical novel, though they are what go most unnoticed. In this sense, the narrator selects the scene almost arbitrarily, purely to put an end to something endless. As she emphasizes in her final sentence, "since all along there had been too many ends to the story, and since they did not end anything, but only continued something, something not formed into any story, I needed an act of ceremony to end the story."

But beyond its immediate effect, this deliberately inadequate ending also evinces something deeper. In its blending of ends and endlessness, it demonstrates how Davis's novel combines – without reconciling – two paradoxical qualities. In *The End of the Story*, and arguably across Davis's stories more broadly, the composition of a fictional form coincides, at all times, with the preservation of "something not formed." After all, any closed circle's circumference still opens up a continuous curve. Closure and openness, answers and questions, fixity and infinity: to these unsettled oppositions we could also add the "written" and its counterpart, the "unwritten." Thus, the novel that Davis's narrator writes is itself encircled, like any novel, by a halo of hypothetical, unfinished books. In this way, the written work retains an internal relation to an idealized, unwritten other:

> I'm afraid I may realize after the novel is finished that what actually made me want to write it was something different, and that it should have taken a different direction. But by then I will not be able to go back and change it, so the novel will remain what it is and the other novel, the one that should have been written, will never be written.

Late in his life, in a series of lectures inspired by his own unwritten novel, Roland Barthes examined Mallarmé's distinction between the "Album" and the "Book." The Book, argued Barthes, aspires to perfection – it aims to provide an accurate "representation of the universe, homologous to the world." To create such an artwork would be to reflect "the totality of reality and history, from the perspective of transcendence." The Album, by contrast, remains rooted within reality, rather than striving to stand outside it. The world as rendered by the Album is incomplete and chaotic; "not-one, not-ordered, scattered, a pure interweaving of contingencies, with no transcendence." Needless to say, neither Barthes nor Mallarmé crudely confuses these two entities with actual literary texts. The binary is not taxonomical but conceptual; the push and pull between these two poles shapes the production of literary works. On the one hand, the Album and all its manifestations: the fragment, the essay, the unfinished effort. On the other, the Book and its corollaries: the summa, the opus, the completed oeuvre.

But Davis's book complicates this dichotomy: it can be read

either as a ceremonially "ended" story, or an enigmatically endless one. More than this, though, maybe the novel dissolves these very distinctions. "It is strange," remarks Valéry, "how the passage of time turns every work – and so every man – into fragments." He then notes, "nothing whole survives, just as a recollection is never anything more than debris, and only grows sharper through false memories." In encompassing the far points of this passage – exposing its own relentless corrosion, while charting its sharpened refinement – perhaps Davis's novel reveals the paradoxical *brevity* of the long form. Likewise, maybe her writings should not be divided into a "novel" and a set of "stories," but seen instead as stars in a constellation, or points upon a continuum. If this is so, then *The End of the Story*'s accomplishment is to span, with startling simplicity, the full width of writing's spectrum – projecting an image whose clarity is consonant with its decay. "The future of the Book is the Album," writes Barthes, "just as the ruin is the future of the monument." His following metaphor reads like a perfect description of Davis's novel; few figures capture it quite so well:

The book is destined to become debris, an erratic ruin; it is like a sugar cube dissolving in water. Some parts sink; others remain upright, erect, crystalline, pure, and brilliant.

The Other Life That Is Ours

Dawn Raffel, *In the Year of Long Division*

Between 1977 and 1995, the American publishing industry witnessed a burst of avant-garde activity whose cultural impact has yet to be adequately assessed. The years in question correspond to the legendary (and controversial) career of Gordon Lish as senior editor for fiction at Alfred A. Knopf. For nearly two decades Lish was uniquely placed to, as he put it, "indulge my fantasies at the expense of a large corporation." And in retrospect, the situation does seem somewhat fantastical: during Lish's tenure, a major corporate publisher financed and distributed an unprecedented – and since unsurpassed – efflorescence of dense, difficult, undoubtedly loss-making works of art. From Diane Williams to Gary Lutz, Rudy Wilson to Jason Schwartz, Lish championed writers who challenged fundamental conventions of style and form. He also fought on behalf of first-time authors – in his words, "the young and unsung" – as well as short story collections, a notable number of them by women.

Of these, Dawn Raffel's *In the Year of Long Division* deserves special attention. First published in 1995, this collection was among the last of Lish's commissions to come out from Knopf; he was fired while it was in the final stages of production. Praised in its day, but long since out of print, Raffel's debut has been hidden from view for too many years. It remains read, of course – whether as a reward for fans who follow the trail back from Raffel's later books (such as 2012's *The Secret Life of Objects*), or as a fixture on the second-hand shopping lists of Lish-obsessives like me. But in its own way, this book deserves just as far-reaching a renaissance as that recently enjoyed by, say, Renata Adler's *Speedboat*. For this reason, serious readers will welcome its return as part of Dzanc's e-book-only "rEprint" series. Since

2011, Steven Gillis and Dan Wickett at Dzanc have brought a wealth of such rarities back into (so to speak) "print," many of which are from Lish's list: the series includes increasingly hard-to-find titles by Patricia Lear, Sam Michel, Michael Martone, and more.

So, Raffel is an author associated with what some have called the "School of Lish." Yet this crude category does a disservice to what are often – both thematically and stylistically – strikingly singular writers and works. To be sure, Raffel's stories do share some common ground with those of other Lish-influenced authors: their focus on uncomfortable "family romances" recalls the contemporaneous early works of Christine Schutt and Yannick Murphy; their rootedness in a provincial, lower middle-class locale (here, an inhospitable Midwest) could even evoke Raymond Carver. In reality, though, Raffel's writing ranges far wider than this. Her distinctive approach to dialogue, for instance – with speech patterns shattered by pauses, impasses, and pregnant omissions – appears directly indebted to Pinter. And although Lish taught his students to treat the sentence as the ultimate unit of composition, Raffel's sentences never risk clotting into constraints; the rhythms of her prose are too free and fragmentary to permit too much syntactic restriction.

In the Year of Long Division contains sixteen "short stories" – a label which signally fails to capture the cryptic, elliptical poetry that these pieces arrange on the page. It is not that Raffel's fictions don't possess plots – "The Trick" tells the tale of a troubled marriage; "We Were Our Age," a dysfunctional childhood friendship – it is more that the substance of these stories is inseparable from the style of their telling. Flaubert once wrote to Louise Colet that, for him, "a good prose sentence must be like a good line of verse... as rhythmic, as sonorous." What he meant was not that he privileged style over substance, but that he sought to dissolve the distinction between the two: to make style the mirror of writing's meaning. What drove Flaubert also drives Raffel – for both, the ideal "story" is one whose content can't be divorced from its form. And also like Flaubert, Raffel has remarked that she shapes her sentences by reading them aloud. Consequently, in their sonority, they sing of the things that speech alone can't express.

For instance, a Raffelian phrase like "the ice, I see, is swept, wet, white" seems to achieve, in its fluid assonance, the physical *form* of a frozen lake; in its frictionless flow from one vowel to the next, the sentence itself skates across the surface it so tactilely describes. In precisely this way, Raffel's writing clings closely to sensory surfaces, calibrating language to the contours of a world which can't clearly be spoken of. Her work eschews information in favor of mystery – we never quite know what is happening, or to whom; rather, the very style of these stories evokes an *experience* of unknowing. As one of her characters puts it, "the trick is not to think" – instead, the only rule when reading Raffel is to listen and feel.

In one of the standout stories of this collection, "The Other R's," Raffel literalizes this emphasis on the enigmatic, the unknown. The story is told from the viewpoint of a child, who has heard that a neighboring family, "the R's – the other R's, not us," have "something the matter with their baby." In barely eight pages of spare, precise prose, Raffel reduces us, as readers, to her young narrator's condition of not-knowing. Even the house of the "other R's" is "draped, tight, tucked in," all closed doors and drawn curtains. Accordingly, like the narrator, we are "made to snoop" – to pry, to eavesdrop, all to no avail. We even get a glimpse of the baby carriage – "a dark, hooded thing," before which we "hang back to watch; quiet, drawn." In Raffel's hands, such details circle around an event that is never explained, only subjected to an evolving opacity.

In this sense, the "division" suggested by this book's title describes the disunity between an always partial, perspectival knowledge and an unknowable truth. And in so doing – as Raffel herself has remarked in an interview – it also speaks to "the divide between feeling and language; between the vastness of our experience and the tiny fraction of it that finds its expression in speech." Indeed, Raffel's fractured rendering of spoken language is one of her most remarkable feats. The full, disorienting effect can only be captured by quoting a passage at length – this dialogue comes from the collection's eleventh story, "Nightjars":

> She offered him something. "Eat," she said.
> "Vern?" she said.
> "What now?" he said.
> "Do you think there's a heaven?"
> Under his notes, he held it still.
> "Ask me what I think," she said.
> "Do you want to hear something true?" he said.
> "Don't know," she said. "Depends." She crossed her arms.
>   Her knees she brought up chestwise.
> His jaw was slowly working. "I never liked to travel," he said.
> "That so?"
> "It is."
> "Myself, I would say it depends," she said.
> "Would you?"
> "I would."
> "What on?"
> "How far," she said.
> "To where?"
> She expelled her breath.
> "Bad answer," she said.

The conversation is classic Raffel: stuttering, stunted, and sharply disjunctive – but, for these reasons, uncompromisingly naturalistic. To adopt a Freudian term, Raffel's treatment of speech is *uncanny*; it is radically confusing precisely because of its resemblance to reality. This is speech as it is spoken in life, not in literature: shorn of explanatory apparatus, driven more by conflicting agendas than by semantics, and, in its resultant asymmetry, rife with abrupt about-turns and non-sequiturs. In Raffel, talk is not novelistic, but chaotically quotidian; as she writes elsewhere in this collection, "all the talk in our town was talk, talk, talk. That, no this. Rain, no shine. More, no less."

Crucially then, the bewilderment we experience when reading Raffel's spoken exchanges is that of encountering an alien language – only to realize it is our own. Or rather, it is our language, but distanced, defamiliarized: Raffel's conversations are clearly intelligible to their participants, but not to us, since we are refused access to the shared context that surrounds them – to what Wittgenstein would call their "form of life." In this respect, perhaps there are *two* languages at play in Raffel; that of speech and that of life, where the latter remains intractably silent. So, precisely as Pinter puts it, "this speech is speaking of a language locked beneath it. That is its continual reference. The speech we hear is an indication of that which we don't hear."

This is the crux of Raffel's accomplishment in her early and late work alike. Throughout all of these stories, what is heard, spoken or seen only hints at its flipside: an ineffable reality that exists everywhere around us, but remains beyond reach of our words; beyond sense. "There is another world," Yeats once wrote, "but it is in this one." And this is the secret, silent world that Raffel's work opens onto: the other life that is ours. If there is a message in these stories, it is that life's meaning is most apparent when looked at askance. As Raffel writes, "there is a way that whatever you turn away from owns your heart." Hers is writing with its back turned to what it tells of – but in this very act of turning away it realizes an indirect revelation.

In illustration, it's instructive to return to that earlier image of *ice* – an element that, more than any, seems emblematic of Raffel's art. *In the Year of Long Division* is fascinated by frozen water; by its combination of surface and depth, solidity and concealed liquidity. In "Somewhere Near Sea Level," the "curve and grace" of ice-skating quickly collapses into the "flat flung limbs" of a fall. "Two If By Sea" starts with a girl "testing, toeing, slipping" across an ice-covered river: "just before she went under, she could hear it crack." For me, such moments express the essence of Raffel. Her style slides with weightless grace across the surface of the world. But in so doing, it also puts pressure on that surface, revealing the water that silently waits on its underside. Through this movement, her writing gestures towards the source of its beauty, just as her stories' shortness allows them to touch on astonishing expanses of experience. In the words of one of her narrators, "our lake was great. Could have been an ocean. Under the surface, everything shone."

Pratfall into the Infinite

Lars Iyer, *Dogma*

It might be a little misleading to say that Lars Iyer's *Dogma*, the sequel to *Spurious*, picks up where its predecessor left off. The problem is, *Spurious* made a point of not going anywhere to begin with. Both books are obsessed with "the end times," but their apocalypse seems to be one in which, as Walter Benjamin once observed, "things keep going on as they are."

Hence, *Dogma* sees Iyer's anti-heroes, the "failed philosophers" Lars and W., repeating the same comic routines that caught our attention the first time around. Although the book begins with a trip overseas, and ends with W. losing his job, he and Lars haven't come far from their stock repertoire of "smut, chimp noises and made-up German." Unlike proper protagonists, this dissolute duo don't grow, or change, or learn from their mistakes. Their author isn't interested in character arcs that culminate in completed identities. Yet if neither Lars nor W. go on a "journey," then that's what makes their story significant: theirs is an unplotted pratfall into the infinite. In other words, Iyer's writing leads us away from what we're led to expect from literature. Indeed, it seems to suggest that failing to live up to literature may be a means of overcoming it.

So we mustn't misread either of Iyer's books as "literary fiction," in any straightforward sense. Here we're dealing with something laughably less than literature – but maybe, therefore, something more. In a recent manifesto, Iyer has argued that literature is "dead," and that trying to write it today is a kind of imposture. If this is so, *Dogma*'s response is to mockingly mark its own imposture, showing up its shortage of literary seriousness. Thus there's a moment when W. likens himself and Lars to "the man and boy of *The Road*, pushing a shopping cart down an empty highway." However, he claims, "in our case... it'll be two men, squabbling over whose turn it is to ride the cart." What he means is that an entire literary ethos, an outlook on life, has been lost. In literature's wake, writing must be made aware that it no longer measures up: "we may have forgotten how to live," says Lars later on, "but they – the authors in W.'s man bag – have not."

Ironic jokes in which literature is both scoffed at and longed for: these will be familiar fare for anyone who's read *Spurious*. As before, the bathos is perfectly pitched, and Lars and W.'s antics are gloriously uproarious. But does *Dogma* succeed in making a more serious statement of failure? That is, can it somehow slough off a "false" literariness by pointedly falling short of it? Interviewed in the run-up to *Dogma*, Iyer called for critics to call the book's bluff:

> I'd like to see a backlash for *Dogma*... I dream of a detailed takedown... something really *cruel*... I have a desire to be *told off*, to be *not allowed to get away with it*. A desire for the order of the world to be restored, even as I know that it cannot be restored. This, of course, is really the desire for an older literary world, a world of tradition and security from which I feel utterly estranged...

I'd say such a takedown should start by attacking the terms in which this appeal is framed. Iyer implies that a better or "older" world, where literature could still exist, would be one where his own writing couldn't. The presumption here is that *Spurious* and its sequel are "signs of the times," and thus that books can still sum up the epoch in which they're written: surely a "literary" aim, if ever there was one. Perhaps Iyer's is a literary project *par excellence*. Presenting his novels as symptoms or symbols, he slightly uncritically slips into sync with one of W.'s dictums in *Dogma*: "always write as though your ideas were world-historical."

Indeed, *Dogma* doesn't try to overturn the true cornerstone of traditional literature: a commitment to the expression of history. It's telling that the book's characters call themselves "harbingers," as W. has it. "That we're alive," he announces, "is a sign of the nearness of the end." The personal accusations that W. levels at Lars further cement the pair's representativeness. If bad things are happening in history, they're happening "in you above all," he reminds him; whatever's wrong with the world is always wrong "with *you*." In this sense, Iyer's characters embody the qualities that the critic Georg Lukács admired in Tolstoy's creations. As Lukács would say, Lars and W. are "typologically" embedded in their historical setting. Whether this is good or bad isn't the issue. The point is that it's quintessentially *literary*. So if Iyer would like to imply that his writing arrives "after literature," then its arrival is already complicated by an unexamined literariness.

Literature is hard to have done with, and Iyer isn't the first to exaggerate a report of its death. But if *Dogma* doesn't fully succeed in failing to *be* literature, what, in its failed failure, might it begin to become? Iyer has elsewhere espoused the idea that writers should cultivate their "legitimate strangeness." Well, what *Dogma* does is deepen the strangeness of *Spurious*. Instead of resolving the earlier work's contradictions, it only makes them more involved, more intractable. We've seen how it sets itself up to fail, then fails to do that. In so doing, it doesn't so much plumb the depths as discover a deeper depthlessness. So, *Dogma* gives us a growing sense that the strangeness of Iyer's work is "legitimate," precisely because it pursues but can't achieve illegitimacy.

Somewhere around the anticlimactic end of this novel, W. advocates an activity called "non-thinking." The "non-" in this coinage is "not privative," he claims. For him the expression "means something more than a simple negation." In the same sort of vein, we could say that *Dogma*'s double failure starts to show us what a "non-literature" might look like. If Iyer's writing never completely negates literature, neither does it naively affirm it. Instead it pulls us toward a place that isn't quite "after" literature, but that somehow subsists both inside and outside of it. Of course, you needn't agree with me to enjoy *Dogma*'s jokes, or to appreciate its superbly accomplished absurdity. But beneath all that, there is, I think, something important at work in the book. Or rather, something which stops working, which breaks down, and which ends up presenting writing itself as an unsolvable problem.

The Background Noise of the Universe

Tor Ulven, *Replacement*

Published two years before Tor Ulven's suicide, *Replacement* has been billed as the Norwegian author's only "novel." But this word doesn't adequately define a book which eschews familiar narrative features; one which immerses us in a storyless world. *Replacement* is about the banal, not the novelistic. It's a work in which, as one character says, "nothing stands out any more than anything else." Nothing is artificially emphasized; all is equally weighted, whether people or things, or even the most micro-scopic physical processes. The end result is less like reading a novel than listening in on the background noise of the universe.

The book begins with a description of a draft of air parting a pair of curtains. Light is let in through a slit, then shut out, leaving darkness. Then light, then darkness, again and again. Before anyone appears on the scene, there is only an anonymous motion – a breath that lies behind light and dark, life and death, such that each of these states is purely "provisional." This tableau sets the tone of the text as a whole. What follows is a flow of words in which characters come into being only to collapse, their voices rising and falling before being replaced. Pronouns slip from "he" to "you" to "she" to a second, italicized "*she*," cease-lessly switching perspective. But beneath this broken string of personae lies a single life-giving movement, like the breeze that blows open those curtains.

In *Replacement*, the personal is preceded by the elemental; everyone is embedded in their environment. A character contem-plates flashes of lightning, and then looks at X-rays of his body. "You could examine the X-rays in the glow of the lightning," he considers. "Perhaps the electricity could make the skeleton come alive." After all, the energy we see in the sky is the same stuff that streams through our nervous systems. In this sense, subject and object can't stand apart – what we observe is what animates us; our world is what we are made of. Later, a pair of "faded bicycle tracks" are likened to "the twisted rope-ladder shape of a DNA molecule." Here a metaphorical leap is made by the mind's eye, yet we're reminded that this mind is made from the same "molecules" it imagines. Consciousness may impose meaning on nature, but nature must first create consciousness. Thus, beneath these fragmentary thoughts and feelings, we glimpse what one character calls the "genetic truth" of our origins – the way we're all formed from the same raw materials.

But while *Replacement* reveals our natural roots, it never leaves nature naively idealized. Indeed, nature always withdraws from ideals. Whenever a character comes across natural beauty, like when one sees shapes on the face of the moon, we're bluntly reminded that such patterns possess "no real shape at all." So, although *Replacement* reflects an aesthetic awareness of the world – an intense attention to the way life looks and feels – nothing is ever painted over or prettified. In this respect *Replacement* is far from "romantic," far from some serenely pastoral appreciation of nature. In fact its tone is at times unpredictably critical, not merely meditative; more active than poetically passive. Some of the book's most astonishing moments come when a contemplative voice acquires an angry or agitated edge. One rant against bankers ruthlessly berates "those dour, obsessive-compulsive, humorless pricks." In *Replacement*, perception refuses to stop at beauty, being equally alive to bracing ugliness. To truly witness the world involves friction; sometimes we're left feeling inflamed.

It's often unclear whether Ulven's voices are meant to be many, or one. They certainly speak and think of similar things. Like Beckett's creations, all are crippled, decrepit, or otherwise waning. Decay, says one, is the "lowest multiple," which may be why these characters seem to converge. In their infirmity, each shares something essentially human. As it's put at one point, "people are only really revealed in decline." Yet if decay and decline disclose the human condition, they also herald a kind of heroism. Early on, we meet an old man for whom "unbuttoning a shirt is a real task… a project in itself… a triumph every time." *Replacement* is full of such everyday struggles. But because the book balances all events equally, compressing life's major and minor moments, these delicate acts acquire a heartrending resonance.

Other epiphanies come when characters blur and melt into each other, into their surroundings, or both. Such scenes seem suffused with what Freud would call an "oceanic" emotional oneness. Two lovers trace the shadows of their hands along a wall, until the silhouettes "meet in secret… as if some unrecognized part of you had met some unrecognized part of her… in a place neither of you knew about." Later on, *Replacement*'s most lyrical section sees another couple (they could be the same) strolling through a field. They pause, he holds her foot, and she empties a pebble from her shoe:

> Through your hand you could feel the warmth of her foot, and you watched the sunlight on the waving grass, and suddenly you felt as if you were a live wire, a relay… you were the connection between the reserve of beauty in her and the straightforward, endlessly complex reality around you, beginning with the sunlit grass and ending everywhere and nowhere. Did the landscape's late summer light come from her or did her warmth come from the sun? Both.

Yet once the revelation is over, *Replacement* returns us to the ground underfoot, to reality as it is before we're aware of it. Summer fields are soon replaced by fossilized skeletons, by driftwood, detritus, and all of life's "deafening biological racket." This too, Ulven tells us, is truth. The true world, a dying voice claims as the book closes, is one where "if we'd never been born it'd make no difference." Like life itself, *Replacement* is full of both beauty and suffering. Finally though, it feels full of something far beyond both. It's filled with as much of the blind will of the world as any book can capture. But what we learn from it is that we're bound to the world, and that the world is what binds us together.

Difficult Intimacies

Christine Schutt, *Prosperous Friends*

Pick up a book by Christine Schutt, and you'll be struck straight away by her style. Praised by the likes of Lydia Davis and John Ashbery, Schutt has been called a "writer's writer." In two short story collections and three novels, she's honed a language that feels wholly hers: a carefully cadenced poetic prose which warrants being read reverently, aloud. I'll say it right now: I believe *Prosperous Friends* proves Schutt to be one of the finest stylists alive. Yet if her style is "writerly," it's not narrow-mindedly so. She isn't indulging in insular word games, fashioned for a refined few. What matters is what she *does* with her words. And what she does is draw out a secret world of love and suffering, which, once we're shown it, we know is our own.

Schutt's first collection, *Nightwork*, disclosed these secrets with such disturbing directness that critics tagged it as "trans-gressive," a briefly trendy genre marker back in the 90s. Broadly, this was a book about incest. Its feral Freudian stories staged a return of our most repressed urges – those unacknowledged desires that underlie our relationships with our nearest and dearest. It was also a book born under the guidance of Gordon Lish, whose workshops Schutt went to by day while writing by night, and who later commissioned the collection for Knopf. Looking back, *Nightwork* seems stamped by what Lish demanded from his students: an arresting extremity of style and subject matter.

Lish's influence can likewise be felt in Schutt's first novel, *Florida*. *Florida* was about an abandoned girl's growth into adulthood, and her adoption of art – of writing – as a way of saving herself. As in *Nightwork*, the novel enacted a kind of confession: an articulation of private and painful experience. In workshops, Lish would urge writers to unearth their innermost "errors," their failures, as sources of power on the page. Thus, *Florida*'s first-person perspective fully uncovers its narrator's mind, so that, in reading, we relive her psychic losses and gains.

But by the time of Schutt's second novel, *All Souls*, something had changed. The shock tactics of *Nightwork* had gone, as had *Florida*'s self-consciousness. An omniscient narrator mediates *All Souls*' action, lending a sense of distance to Schutt's story of two schoolgirls. *Prosperous Friends* continues this trend, observing its characters' lives largely from outside. So, where secrets were once spilled onto the page, now they're withheld, or else merely whispered. To me though, it seems that Schutt's early concerns have only grown more movingly present. All the more present, that is, for their apparent absence. The more they withdraw, the more their mystery deepens. In short, Schutt has mastered an intricate *indirectness*.

After all, her art is partly about unspoken emotions, and the clandestine life of the body. So we could say that with each new book this bodily, emotive life is ever more expertly buried. Now it lives less in Schutt's themes than her forms; less in plots than in prosody. Difficult intimacies no longer need explicit confession. Instead they're secreted in Schutt's very sentences – coded in consonance, assonance, syllabic patterning. Another great writer, Gary Lutz, has lectured at length on the "romance between letters" in Schuttian phrases like "her lips stuck when she licked them to talk" and "acutely felt, clearly flat." This is why reading her prose is like listening to music. Beneath its manifest meaning, her language is full of other, ineffable messages, encrypted in rhythms and melodies. Literary critic George Steiner, writing about music, explains the effect better than I can – this is what it's like to read Schutt:

The sensory, emotional data of music are far more immediate than those of speech... they may reach back to the womb.

Music needs no decipherment. Reception is more or less instantaneous at psychic, nervous and visceral levels whose synaptic interconnections and cumulative yield we scarcely understand.

It's appropriate, then, that *Prosperous Friends* opens with its main character crying. As with a child, we hear her cries – a kind of primal music – before we come to hear her speech. Isabel Bourne's "exorbitant crying" awakens Aura Kyle, proprietor of the B & B where Isabel has checked in overnight with her husband Ned. Straight away, Aura attempts to interpret the noises she hears. What could have caused her guest's anguish? "Infidelity? Boredom?" No, there's no way of knowing: this is a voice as it was before learning language, expressive only of emotion, of "purely announced sorrow." Two sentences follow, forming a startling simile of the sort only Schutt could come up with:

Her swept, stripped crying was like an empty room, the boxy shadows on the walls, the unfaded parts against which beds and desks had pressed. Whoever had lived there, slept there, adjusted in front of a mirror there, was dead.

In a sense, Isabel's inner "deadness" marks the difference between her and Ned. Her husband's first word in the novel is "feel" – he's involved in the world, "up for anything," while Isabel is ill at ease in it. She looks out at others as if "through a window," and is predisposed to "shift into remote." As soon as we meet these two, *in medias res*, their marriage already seems ruined. But Schutt refuses easy readings; like Isabel's crying, we can't reduce this couple's collapse to a "cause." Rather, the relationship's dissolution is due to some unsounded under-current – an abstract "absence of event," paraphrased at one point as "Isabel's failure to make something worth regarding."

For sure, she's a thwarted writer, and not only that: an abortion darkens her past, as well as allusions to an "ashy collapse."

What's more, this husband and wife's sex life is more unnerving than anything in *Nightwork*. Ned tries his hardest to be inventive with Isabel, whether "rustling up her skirt" in a church, encouraging her to experiment with girls, or to "let me shave you." For all his efforts, she "can only act excited." He finds her desires unfathomable. What would she like him to do for her, to her? "If only she knew, but she never." Their vexed sex scenes end in deadlock: he needs to know what she needs, but there's no way of knowing, for either of them. This is a subtler, deeper discomfort than that of Schutt's more extreme early stories – like *Dead Men*, where a remembered lover has a "long reach for hard objects," and declares "you could take my fist, you cunt." Now the urge to abuse has given way to something strangely worse: misguided bids to gratify. The writing that results is elliptical, but all the more excruciating:

> "How do you like this?"
> "Yes, well. No, not exactly."
> "How about this?"
> "Yes."
> "This?"
> "A little."
> "This?"
> "No. No, that hurts. That really hurts, Ned!"
> Afterward, the only thing he could say was that he wanted to give her pleasure.
> "Not that way, you don't."
> She showered in a plugged-up tub, then sat growing colder in the scum that was water.

Isabel is far from frigid, although her husband might make her seem so. She has burning needs of her own, but they're unknown, unknowable. And if a cloud of unknowing surrounds her desire, the same could be said of her depression. "I'm depressed," she tells Ned, "but the reason? You don't know the reason, not really." For her, in fact, pain and pleasure are never completely distinct. "I like melancholy," she claims, and later quotes *The Great Gatsby*: she's "both enchanted and repelled" by the world, and by herself. Most of us know how she feels, at least a little. As psychoanalysts have long held, enchantment and repulsion meet and merge on the underside of our emotional lives. But Isabel is immersed in this netherworld, out of sight of the surface.

The consequence is that she can't articulate how she feels, only feel it. Thus she identifies with a blind, deaf dog which Ned gets put down. She, like him, is "purely a heart... a beating heart," insensible but alive and in pain. In this, her condition recalls Julia Kristeva's description of "melancholia." For Kristeva, chronic depression is "incommunicable." Melancholics can't connect feelings with reasons, can't sum up their suffering in speech. Like Isabel, they're locked out of "symbolic" language – their words slip away from fixed points of reference. Instead, their verbal world is what Kristeva calls "the semiotic," where words are submerged in emotions, in inexplicable bodily drives. This is Isabel's realm, but not only that; it's also the place of what could be called, with Steiner, linguistic "music," poetry. So, if you think the plot of *Prosperous Friends* sounds pedestrian, listen closer. Semiotic, not solely symbolic, the book's beating heart lies hidden beneath its ostensible "sense."

On Kristeva's account, there's clearly an ambiguity at the core of depression. In their inarticulate plight, perhaps depressives are like failed artists, blocked writers. But by accessing an inner world of poetic expression, each is also an artist in the making. This is why Kristeva claims that "depression is at the threshold of creativity." If it "becomes creative," she goes on, "it is overcome." So the condition contains the seed of its cure. One way of recovering from melancholia is to craft an "independent symbolic object" – a work of art. Seen in this light, *Prosperous Friends* tells the story of Isabel's struggle to cross such a threshold. As we will see, her failure is brought into focus by others' success.

The prosperous friends of Schutt's title are two artists, Clive and Dinah, an older couple whose country home Ned and Isabel flee to during the dying days of their marriage. Isabel has a half-hearted affair with Clive; Ned finally leaves her for the latter's niece-in-law, Phoebe. Clive is a painter, Dinah a poet, and each is forever engaged in fertile work of one kind or another: "Dinah had a garden... Poems? They grew." For all their flaws their love flourishes too: they still have good sex (unlike Isabel and Ned) and have learned to accept each other's infidelities. This isn't to say that they're free from sorrow. Dinah and Clive are as acquainted with pain as the book's younger couple, but they sublimate it in their everyday lives, and their art. One of Clive's most well-known works depicts white horses, painted after an injury, "in response to a moment when pain felled him and the world was white." Even if pain can't be comprehended, it can be conquered in painting.

When Ned leaves unannounced in the night, Isabel has no such hope of coping. Once abandoned, she is "broken." Her marriage, or at least its image, is all that has kept her from collapse. "From the girl most promising," we learn, "she had not been a success, except outwardly in marriage. And now the marriage was over." Without this symbolic lynchpin, she no longer knows herself. Or, more exactly, she's lost her excuse for believing she ever had. Her motives are now as opaque to her as they are to others. This crisis culminates in a car crash, after which Clive asks if she "drove off the road on purpose." She replies, "I don't know. I don't remember feeling involved."

Ultimately, all Isabel knows is that she's "not turning into the person I wanted to be." Her sadness at what she hasn't become rings true to life, and is tragic. But the real, irreparable tragedy is that this sadness is something no one can touch. Ned couldn't, and neither can Clive, for whom Isabel is simply a "shape," an inscrutable surface. By contrast, Clive and Dinah are open, not closed, to their own and each other's limitations. They, too, are saddened by what they are not. Yet this self-same sadness is what cements them together. People are imperfect, as is art, and such failings have to be acknowledged. Hence, one of the book's most moving moments comes when Clive quotes his wife's poetry to her:

> His recall for her work mostly pleases and when they come to the barn bench, he is still plucking lines, and she is listening to herself and how he hears her, and it wins her over that he knows, better than anyone else knows, the great divide between who she is and what she has done.

For couples like Clive and Dinah, divides and abysses are bridged, thresholds crossed, in these small acts of acceptance.

Prosperous Friends does end with a hint of hope for Isabel, who arrives at a dawning relationship with Clive's daughter, Sally. To be sure, Sally is almost as sad as Isabel, with her "happy pills" and "AA meetings." But together the two show signs of being able to share their sadness, as Isabel never could with Ned. In Dinah's words, "there may be cures to loneliness, but marriage is not one of them." Isabel and Sally's future is uncertain, but we sense that it won't be, or needn't be, lonely. They're still at the stage where, as Sally says of two strangers they see at a dance, "they might be anything to each other." When we leave them watching those dancers – "they hopped and clapped, hooked arms, went in circles" – the book seems to return to its source: a wordless world of musical movement and uncertain, bittersweet beauty.

Prosperous Friends is a book about how some lives take shape, and some fail to. It's also a work of art about how art can bring shape to our lives. Lastly, it shows us how sharing, in life and in art, can overcome sadness. This thought brings us back to Kristeva, who says of despair that "our job is to raise it to the level of words, and of life." In this way, perhaps Schutt raises and redeems the desperate lives she portrays. She doesn't plot those lives, but looks into them indirectly, evocatively. Her poetic sentences speak of the things they can't say, disclosing unknowable love and pain. And all this is brought forth, given shape, by the work in which it is contained. A last allusion might underline this novel's accomplishment. At some point, Sally discovers a book about jigsaws. The book is real; it's by Margaret Drabble. Read it, and you'll find the following words:

> Books, too, attempt to impose a pattern, to make a shape. We aim, by writing them, to make order from chaos. We fail.

It isn't so much that Schutt succeeds in making order from chaos. She knows that she can't, we can't, no one can. So she says, once you've failed, go on living: make order from failure.

The Impenetrable Everyday

Enrique Vila-Matas, *Dublinesque*

Dublinesque is the story of Samuel Riba, retired publisher, recovered alcoholic, and more importantly someone for whom "reading is a way of being in the world, an instrument for interpreting day to day life." On the brink of his sixtieth birthday Riba plots a trip to Dublin, prompted by "a strange, premonitory dream" he had while almost fatally ill two years earlier. There he hopes to perform "a funeral for the age of print, for the golden age of Gutenberg," loosely based on a literary model: Paddy Dignam's funeral in chapter six of Joyce's *Ulysses*.

The funeral acts as the focal point for an elision of life and literature – a writerly ritual where the mundane is remade as metaphor. So, although Riba is described as a "publisher," in *Dublinesque* this is not a job title. Instead it denotes an inner disposition, "an exaggerated fanaticism for literature" which would put Riba at odds with much of the book trade today. In fact, *Dublinesque* has almost nothing to do with publishing, and Riba's grief for the passing of print's "golden age" isn't cultural commentary; it's largely a grief for his own lived losses, and for "everything that, with time, he'd come to see was buried."

Riba's journey to Dublin is therefore a journey inward, "to the very center of his dream." Indeed, it's not just that Riba's "real" journey is determined by the dream that precedes it. Rather, we sense that he's still asleep, perhaps even already dead – either way, the dream never ended. He seems forever immersed in *reverie*, whether relapsing into drunkenness, reminiscing, or dissociatively surfing the internet. Hence, his dream is less an event that sets his story in motion, more a horizon within which it occurs. To reach its center would be for him to achieve what Jung called "individuation" – knowing himself anew, as when one first looks in a mirror. What's more, it would also mean writing a story, whose words would all indirectly refer to himself – the sort of story written in dreams and forgotten on waking. In this respect Riba is, as Freud said of writers, "a dreamer in broad daylight."

For Riba, then, to live is to dream is to write is to read. For better or worse, he can't detach these terms from each other. This is why his inner life, and his narrative voice, consist of "an accumulation of literary quotations," an intertextual tissue where countless writers – Larkin, Gracq, Auster, almost anyone – coexist in a "tangled mess," their words and his rendered inextricable. Yet while *Dublinesque* is densely referential, it is emphatically not a "postmodern" novel. Its practices of collage and pastiche don't purport to connect to any collective condition. Instead, and more enigmatically, literature is a private language through which Riba relates to himself. His references rely on an associative freight accrued for him alone. For him, literature is wholly embedded in lived experience; his allusions are only intelligible in terms of his *habitus*. So, although the book implies infinite literary linkages, this is a bounded infinity, fully enclosed – less like an intertext than an inexplicable dream.

Describing a dream is like describing another person; in each case, the object withdraws from observation. The interiors of people and dreams are fractal: like Mandelbrot's coastlines, they can't be conclusively mapped. With *Dublinesque*, the same can be said of the novel. Near the beginning of the book, Riba's father refers to "the unfathomable dimension," a remark which recurs whenever Riba encounters something "inextinguishable, unreachable." He detects this dimension in great literature, but also in "the grey rhythm of the prosaic," the inscrutable details of daily life. In Walter Benjamin's words, we could say *Dublinesque* is entangled in "the everyday as impenetrable, the impenetrable as everyday." Because of this, the book itself becomes unaccountable, exceeding the reach of our reading.

Whenever it briefly clears into coherence, an alien phrase or fragment will arise as if from nowhere, returning us to total estrangement. To take one example: "even the rain beneath which all the dead once fell in love will have faded away."

The problem presented by *Dublinesque* is one of orientation. How are we to find our feet within an unfathomable work? Of course, this is also the problem that *Ulysses* poses – it is, in a sense, Joyce's challenge to literature. With Joyce, maybe more than with any author before him, the literary work appears to require a literary theory. Not only this, but *Ulysses* sets out to prove that a work can theorize itself through its practice. It does so by means of a complex web of "correspondences," mapping its textual territory with a system of symbols. Indeed, it is almost as if *Ulysses* aims to *exhaust* itself in this internal project of explication. Signs of a similar project can be seen in *Dublinesque*, where Riba seems surrounded by "secret forces" and "metaphorical associations," as if "a code lay concealed behind every scene in his life." But if the book hints at Joycean encryption, it only does so to delight in misleading us. *Dublinesque* does not and cannot contain a map of itself. In this sense it's telling that Riba, too, tries to construct a "theory of the novel." Before long he concludes that "the best thing to do is to travel and to lose theories, lose them all." *Dublinesque* is a work that has built but abandoned its theory. Yet it has let its ruined landmarks stand, the better to lose itself by.

Ultimately, even *Ulysses* fails to fully explain itself, which is why Joyce resorted to the supplementary "schema" he sent to Stuart Gilbert in 1921. Toward its end, *Dublinesque* dovetails with this device, dividing its episodes into sub-headed sections with titles like "time," "style," "action," and "themes." But the effect is not one of rationalization. Joyce's schematic title for chapter six of *Ulysses* was "Hades" – Dignam's funeral is designed to echo Odysseus' descent to the realm of the dead. Perhaps the difference between these books is best grasped through an allegory of death and rebirth. *Ulysses* buries its thematic workings, whereas *Dublinesque* raises them to the surface. The book's most unfathomable mystery lies in the way it insistently spells itself out. Whenever Riba sees a pattern, a parallelism, some figurative flourish, he can't help but refer to it. For him, after all, literature is self-relation. As a result – and this is the real achievement of *Dublinesque* – literature is returned to the realm of experience. The novel is not a puzzle to be solved. It has always and already solved itself, bringing what was buried back to life. This is a book in which things are no longer concealed; where writing and reading revivify whatever we thought was dead inside us. "You haven't come to Dublin to turn yourself into a metaphor, have you?" Riba is asked at one point. "That and so I can feel alive," he replies.

Fractal Baroque

Jason Schwartz, *John the Posthumous*

Conventionally, a review of a novel should offer some sort of synopsis. Such a review might climb to all sorts of interpretive heights, but still, a basic part of its job is to summarize its subject's plot. At an elementary level, reviews are expected to be about what books are "about." And this is precisely where Jason Schwartz's new novel poses a problem. *John the Posthumous* is impossible to synopsize. Put bluntly, this book will beat any critic's attempt to boil it down to a summary. But it doesn't follow from this that the book has no plot. Rather, *John the Posthumous* reminds us as readers that plots aren't reducible to what we can *describe*. Instead, as with crimes or conspiracies, plots can be something we try to *discover* – with no certainty of success.

In this respect, Schwartz's writing spins the reading experience into reverse. His prose puts readers in a position where the most rudimentary aspects of reading are no longer givens, but goals. Our literary traditions train us to want certain "returns" from the task of reading. Usually, we'd like novels to leave us with an enlarged self-understanding; a better idea of where we belong in the world. But Schwartz's work shrinks from the world, like a whirlpool, pulling us down to a depth from which nothing returns to the surface. Or maybe it's more like a dream – one whose meaning can't be translated back into waking language. Whatever the metaphor, this sort of writing frustrates some fundamental assumptions about the consolations of fiction. In short, Schwartz is *difficult*.

John the Posthumous articulates an alien linguistic world, woven together from Biblical quotes, opaque legal cases, and allusions to Winslow Homer's paintings – not to mention eighteenth-century conduct books, histories of the French monarchy, and the floor-plans of abandoned properties (that's just to begin with). The book is a baffling accumulation of folklore and apocrypha, convincing fictions and far-fetched facts. To take one example, Schwartz's narrator cryptically claims that "some Colonial maps display rows of daggers for fenceposts, and rows of cannons for houses." Later he remarks – apparently at random – that "maps of the body, in early anatomy, display the organs as houses in a town." Now, imagine a book built wholly out of such statements; a map that collates other maps – of history, culture, and literature – and then madly scrambles their coordinates. This, for instance, is a typical passage:

> The parable of the bed – I imagine the Bible contains no such item. What delicate phrases we must, therefore, do without. Tin knives and burnt blankets, a plague gate. Buried night-dresses, whether diseased or in pieces, find considerable favor in chronicles of a more Teutonic sort. While the parable of the gown ends, once again, without evidence of my wife.

So far, so impenetrable – but let's take a different tack. Threaded throughout these strange declarations, the words "wife" and "wives" arise thirty-five times. Also, "adultery" and associated words ("adulterer," "adulteress," the Latin *adultera*," and, "to use the legal term... *adulterium*") make twenty appearances. Correspondingly, "cuckold" and "cuckoldry" (which the narrator notably calls "my proper topic") occur on ten occasions. "Bed," "bedsheets," "bedclothes," and "bedroom" combine to a total of ninety. So, it's striking that "knife," "knives," and "blade" add up to sixty-seven. "Blood" appears twenty times, "throat" nineteen, and "murder" and "kill" total twenty again. Forty-four instances of "burn," "burnt," "burning," "fire," and "flame" fan out across the text. Finally, tellingly, there are twenty-one uses of "body," always appearing alongside such phrases as "in agony," "oddly marked," "in distress," "broken," and, of course, "burnt."

Now we're getting somewhere: whether or not Schwartz provides a "plot," he at least leaves a trail of breadcrumbs; a path through the labyrinth. Schwartz's assorted facts and falsehoods hint at a hidden "history of adultery" – or, as the narrator later describes it, "a geometry of nuptial detail." And the pivotal piece of this puzzle – the wife – is unnervingly absent. On one level, then, the book can be read as a killer's confession – perhaps a coded personal journal, peppered with clues; or a rulebook for a meta-literary murder mystery. But Schwartz isn't merely playing games. The power of *John the Posthumous* stems less from the promise of solving a puzzle, more from the emotions evoked when that promise is broken. Ultimately, what the book is "about" can't be reconstructed into a narrative arc. All that's left, then, is the trauma of narrative's aftermath. Not stories, but *feelings* of fragmentation and loss form the lifeblood of *John the Posthumous*.

So, whenever Schwartz seems on the verge of revealing a story – or simply a sense of "progression" – he suddenly swerves, reversing away from revelation. And on closer inspection, this sort of reversal structures the book right down to the sentence level. The narrator's claims nearly always entail either self-contradiction (he describes a scene as "north of the slaughter, or south of it"), equivocation (he calls a character "Edward, or perhaps Edmond"), or painstaking qualification ("or, more precisely" is his favored formula). At one point he declares, "The word adultery derives from *cry*," but then admits that it "does not; just as you had suspected." In this way, his words recoil back into themselves – offering meaning with one hand; occluding it with the other. Hence any semblance of significance is "circled, but also crossed out," to take another of his phrases. What gets left over from this operation – the remainder of Schwartz's equation – is only an outline, an *aura* of an untold story, as in this haunting tableau:

The wife burns the husband's clothing. The husband stands at the end of the corridor, on every floor. Our house was quite plain, I am afraid. Pause here, at the door. Present yourself at the window, as she had, and now remove yourself from view.

First it presents its points of reference, and then it removes them forever: in this, Schwartz's extraordinary style is entirely his own. Yet no writer's style comes from nowhere; even the most striking styles are imprinted by influences, or "precursors," as Harold Bloom puts it. If anyone has played a part in shaping Schwartz's prose, it would be Gordon Lish – the editor who published Schwartz's early stories in *The Quarterly*, and his first book, *A German Picturesque*, through Knopf in the 90s. Lish's term for the recursive technique sketched out above is "consecution" – a way of writing by "walking backwards," as some have described it. Through consecution, writing moves onward by mining what has just been written: each sentence treats the previous one as a store of potential to be unpacked, or subverted. Of course, this is a simplification – the approach encompasses an entire aesthetic philosophy – but suffice to say, there's a logic to Schwartz's manipulations of meaning; a method in his madness.

Robert Musil once said that writing should combine "precision and soul." But Schwartz has perfected his own compound of precision and *menace*. As his narrator proclaims, "ornament, according to one argument, portends death." In *A German Picturesque*, Schwartz had already shown a mastery of minutiae, crafting obsessive descriptions of trinkets – "bracelets," "scrollwork," "a Brussels-lace mantilla" – in order to conjure sadness and wonder from their inconsequence. In fact, Schwartz's authorial gaze is as raptly exacting as Robbe-Grillet's; Lish himself has described his style as "a totalized form of attention." And *John the Posthumous* further intensifies this closeness of focus – only here Schwartz turns his attention to horror. In a sense, every scene is a murder scene; every ornament

– "the rod, the shade, the ring" – an "emblem of betrayal." Alluding to occult codes in old Bibles, the narrator remarks that "Satan appears to the left of every phrase. So goes one old notion." And this is true of *John the Posthumous* too; the devil is in the details:

> In our family Bible: the flyleaf is inscribed in blue ink, in a narrow hand. From husband to wife – followed by a month, a slash, a year. There is a curious break in the number eight. And a mark of sorts, a smudge – a tiny form in the corner of the page.

Perhaps such vignettes speak to the very spirit of *John the Posthumous*. The text's chief achievement is its evocation of vast, expansive emotions – sorrow, dread, religious terror – from the most meagre materials; in Schwartz, each "mark" and "smudge" summons up a whole world. And as readers we lose ourselves in this world, as we would in a labyrinth – only, it is one we can't possibly solve. The closer we get to a sense of its center, the more it withdraws; the more intricate its construction becomes. This is the reason why Schwartz's novel – or better, his devilish stylistic edifice – can't be reduced to a story. Ultimately, it's less like a book than a fractal; a shape whose complexity never diminishes, all the way down to the smallest scale. Gilles Deleuze detected such qualities in the dense ornamentation of baroque art; a style, as he said, whose "twists and turns and folds unfurl all the way to infinity." Fractal baroque: an unfurling art that enfolds us in incomprehension, in fear, but also in irreducible beauty. This would be a fitting description of Schwartz's difficult genius – and of the infinite inner world that his writing inhabits.

Stars and Despair

Gabriel Josipovici, *Hotel Andromeda*

> Since the "it" in our existence cannot be identified, since the
> essence of language is its poverty in the face of it, since one
> cannot hold a mirror to it, since it is the monster in the
> labyrinth and the eternal playmate, one strives for an art
> whose aim is to render the effect of its presence.
> – Charles Simic, *Dime-Store Alchemy: The Art of Joseph Cornell*

How can art address those aspects of life that elude direct
expression? In his remarkable book *Art Matters*, the aesthetic
theorist Peter De Bolla describes his encounter with a particular
painting (Barnett Newman's enormous *Vir Heroicus Sublimis*)
whose powerful presence leaves him "struck dumb." Searching
for words to express this unsettling experience, De Bolla poses a
series of questions. Firstly, he asks, "how does this painting
determine my address to it?" Next, as an aspect of that address,
"how does it make me feel?" Crucially, neither inquiry quite
captures the canvas's enigmatic effect; the nimbus that seems to
surround it. "Beyond these questions," De Bolla reflects, "there
lies the insistent murmur of all great art; the nagging thought
that the work holds something to itself, contains something that
in the final analysis remains untouchable, unknowable."
Consequently, he concludes that the only adequate question
would be "what does this painting *know*?" And this very
question, which the critic Michael Wood has since called "truly
haunting," can also be asked of the ambiguous literary artworks
created by the British author Gabriel Josipovici – whose new
novel concerns the equally enigmatic American artist Joseph
Cornell.

Unlike Newman's painting, the curious "boxes" made by

Cornell can't accurately be described as *great* art, since greatness is clearly not Cornell's concern. On the contrary, Cornell's artistry makes much of little, crafting an uncanny atmosphere from the smallest details. Famously, Cornell assembled his boxes from trivial trinkets; forgotten treasures sifted from the thrift stores of old New York. The resulting constructions – obscure collages like the Medici Slot Machine series, or the Soap Bubble sets – are neither (to use Newman's terms) "sublime" nor "heroic." Far from evoking expansive grandeur, they draw us into a strangely constrained inner world. In some respects, this world is recognizably that of the eccentric, or the neurotic: Cornell's boxes often seem like ornate prison cells, adorned with the signs of a personal sadness. Yet somehow we sense that the source of this sadness is never entirely accessible – whether to us, or even to Cornell himself. Within this world, each twig, each cork, each sequin secretes a strangely illegible signature, so that each box as a whole seems to *speak* to itself, as if in its own unique language. And perhaps this private language resembles the "insistent murmur" described by De Bolla; it raises Cornell's eccentricity to something more significant: *knowledge*, enclosed in a cloud of unknowing.

Cornell's air of mystery has attracted many literary admirers, from Octavio Paz to John Ashbery to Charles Simic, whose sequence of ekphrastic prose-poems, *Dime-Store Alchemy*, could be considered the most effective attempt to bottle up some of that cloud, that aura. Josipovici appears well-acquainted with these precursors, and perhaps it is partly thanks to their inspiration that he has now created his own Cornellian novel, named after a box filled with stars and scraps of paper: *Hotel Andromeda*. Josipovici has written briefly on Cornell before – notably in the allusive short stories "The Principle of Order" and "That Which Is Hidden Is That Which Is Shown; That Which Is Shown Is That Which Is Hidden." However, *Hotel Andromeda* represents his first extended engagement with the artist. Characteristically though, when compared to those earlier sketches, the novel's extent doesn't encumber it with extraneous weight. Josipovici is a writer who prizes "lightness," and his airborne prose never tethers or traps Cornell's art; never encases it in the amber of comprehension. Rather, his narrative subtly circles around its subject, tracing the outlines of a shape which remains, to refer back to De Bolla, "untouchable, unknowable."

In this sense, of course, the book is not only about Cornell, but also about the act of writing: an act which itself, as Barthelme says, entails a state of "not knowing." Such is the situation of *Hotel Andromeda*'s protagonist, Helena, who spends the whole novel absorbed in a struggle with writing's inherent uncertainty. We first encounter Helena in conversation with an elderly neighbor, who quizzes her about her estranged sister, Alice. Helena lives in affluent North London, writing art history books, with the help of her inheritance. Alice has emigrated to war-torn Chechnya, where she works in an orphanage. When were they last in touch? Straight away, this everyday question raises the unnerving specter of writing:

- And you don't write? the old lady asks.
- Not any more, Helena says.
- You don't want to know what she's up to?
- Of course I do, Helena says. But I told you. What's the point? She never answers my letters. Perhaps she never gets them. I don't know. But I can't keep writing into the silence.

But writing as such is always directed into this "silence," just as a letter is sent through the empty air. In this way, Helena's statement seems to apply equally to her unanswered letters and to the book she is trying and failing to write – a book about the life and work of Joseph Cornell. Indeed, the letters themselves are bound up with this book, as their implicit purpose is partly to *justify* its production. By explicating her work on Cornell to Alice in Chechnya, Helena hopes to ease her own fear that it is "absurd to be here, in my comfortable flat, trying to write a book about a dead artist hardly anyone has heard of – while all of that is happening over there." So, Helena's letters to Alice reflect her deeper desire to explain her chosen existence. In this respect, they could even be said to "return" to their sender: each message is meant to confirm the rightness of what it describes, thus underwriting its author's identity. Nevertheless, the assertion of selfhood receives no response from the silence. "I sometimes dream I'm writing to her," Helena remarks to her neighbor. "Telling her about my work. Trying to explain. But even in my dreams she never replies." Life, like writing, addresses itself to the world – and the world does not answer.

Hence, if Helena can't explain herself to her sister, neither can she explain herself to herself. A certain external source of meaning is missing. Such a scenario subtly suggests the crisis that Josipovici has elsewhere described, following Weber, as the "disenchantment of the world" – an archetypically modern condition, in which identities come unanchored, and life is left without a divine guarantee. In fiction, of course, there is no need to state such ideas so directly or grandiosely. As with the conversation quoted above, our ordinary talk already contains an entire epistemology of incompleteness and doubt. Likewise, if Josipovici's novels and stories describe a state of disenchantment, they do not do so by means of didactic pronouncements, but through the most delicate calibrations of theme and form. One common feature of these arrangements has been acutely characterized by the critic Victoria Best:

> From the interlocking scenarios of Josipovici's texts to the inability of his characters to be together or apart, what seems to be missing – and desperately, at times – is the presence of a solid third term standing beyond the binary opposition.

Readers of a Josipovici text often long for some substantive perspective or interpretation that could finally release them from their entanglement with that text, and its refusal to offer up meaning.

Hotel Andromeda creates an apparent candidate for that "third term" in the form of Ed, a Czech acquaintance of Alice, who comes to stay in Helena's home. Ed's unannounced arrival arouses our readerly expectations: is he to be that familiar figure, the foreigner who transforms the life of the tribe? Is he Zeus in disguise; the change-bringing stranger? Like us, Helena hopes that her guest will fulfil this fictional function. However, when pressed, he declares, "I do not want to talk." The nature of his connection to Alice is also left unspoken: were they lovers, perhaps? Or is he lying about having known her at all? Ed never reveals any great revelation, nor reconciles, in Helena's terms, "here" with "over there." His narrative role is not as a mediator of meaning, but a random atom; a broken middle. Further frustrating the stereotype that Ed's arrival implies, Helena doesn't exactly learn lessons from her encounter. After she and Ed have had sex, she kicks him out, prioritizing her right to her property over her morals: "I will throw your stuff onto the pavement and change the locks," she shouts, "because that's how I am." Her words enact an ironic reversal of a conversion experience: far from reaching an ethical peripety, Helena comically reverts to type, conforming to the complacency of her class. Here, "disenchantment" effects a deflation of what would have been the biggest cliché – namely, an alternate plot in which Ed would inspire Helena to finally *write* her book; the very book we hold in our hands!

So, this is a novel that nimbly eludes any overly obvious closure. But what does that have to do with Cornell? Strikingly, Josipovici juxtaposes his descriptions of Helena's life with incomplete extracts from her book – a work which only "exists," after all, in the form of those unfinished fragments. Hence, at its heart, *Hotel Andromeda* poses the question of the connection between a make-believe book and the actual book that depicts it. Crucially though, this question can't quite be settled by seeing the narrative as a *commentary* on Cornell; Helena's interactions with Alice and Ed don't help the reader to *clarify* Cornell's art. In this regard, the relationship between the two books is not simply recapitulative. These entities don't exist in a state of neat integration, but one of reciprocal interruption. As a result, the form of the novel itself becomes discomposed. In a less literal sense than Helena's, Josipovici's book is *unfinished*: it furnishes no final alignment; no Archimedean point to fix our perspective. The total effect of the text, as Best puts it above, is one of intricate "entanglement." Thus, our reading experience is roughly this: we apprehend the work as a whole, but we cannot say whether it is broken, or whether the chaos we see conceals an order beyond our knowledge.

Helena seems to sense something like this when she says, contemplating a photo of Cornell, that its "atmosphere is of a demented silence." The formulation feels precisely right, reflecting the boxes' cryptic blend of serenity and neurosis, freedom and claustrophobia. And in articulating this, her statement also speaks to an impossible aspect of her project. As Simic puts it in one of his poems, Cornell's personality appears so introverted as to be ultimately "unknowable," just as his boxes so often seem "beautiful but not sayable." In Helena's phrasing, "he is an absence, beyond speech," such that "to make him the centre of a narrative would be to distort him," and indeed "if I write a portrait of him 'from the inside,' I'm left feeling that I'm furnishing him with an inside which is not there." Moreover, not only is Cornell himself a kind of black box (so to speak) but so is his art, since no one will ever decisively know "whether what he was making was a way of talking to the world, or to himself." For Helena, this is what finally makes Cornell "so ambiguous," and nowhere is this ambiguity better expressed than in his box of 1954, *Andromeda: Grand Hôtel de l'Observatoire*. Here is Helena's written account of this work of art:

> Are we in heaven, then, among the myths of antiquity, or in the workshop of a Renaissance magus, or in a seedy provincial French hotel? The box is profoundly ambiguous. On the one hand this is the hotel of all hotels, a place in the heavens open to the stars, inside which Andromeda, free and transformed, performs her glorious trapeze acts for ever and ever. But the fact that the name appears in French on all too ordinary notepaper allows a hint of sadness and even despair to seep into this image of life in the heavens, sadness at the hubris of such a name, despair at the thought of the bleak reality of such places which, far from redeeming time, convey only the sense that time has passed them by.

Glory and sadness, stars and despair: the box's "unsayable" truth consists of a combination of contradictory qualities. Within the bounded world of the box, "the sordid and the heavenly, reality and the ideal" are constellated but not reconciled, so that the viewer's gaze moves through that world "as in a Möbius strip, perpetually from one to the other." In this vein, we might even say that the box combines conflicting ideas in its *mind*, much as our own minds can sometimes hold two antithetical thoughts in tension. In other words, this work of art could be said to possess a cognitive power; a kind of *knowledge*, whose nature resides in something like what Adorno once called "the consistent consciousness of non-identity." Not only this, but that non-identical knowledge contains an *existential* component. Specifically, the box seems to "know" something about the complex relation – or rather, to recall Best's word, the "entanglement" – that always links art and life. In biographical terms, for Cornell, this relation was partly one of neurotic wish-fulfilment. As Helena says, Cornell was a classic "case" – a recluse, a loner, "chained to his sick brother and domineering mother." Hence, in crafting his heavenly hotel, he could be construed as "creating an image he could long for but never realize."

Certainly, that would be one kind of reading. However, for Helena (and, we sense, for Josipovici) such statements are finally insufficient. We cannot simply come to rest in a romantic conception of art as redemption. Nor is it adequate to conclude of Cornell that, as Paz writes in his poem, "out of your ruins you have made creations." To be sure, it is tempting to take comfort in such reductive re-enchantments. When we feel completely alone, like Cornell, we often long to *escape* into art. Part of us wants to climb into the box, a little like Cornell's beloved Houdini, hoping to find our freedom within it. And yet the *ethical* content of Cornell's art, and indeed of Josipovici's novel, lies precisely in the frustration of such consolations. What the boxes and the book both provide is, as Helena says, a more testing truth: "a dramatization not of the dream but of both the dream and its source in a life from which there is no escape." Thus, although at first glance the box might look closed, somehow the book illuminates the openness of that closure. And while I suspect that what I have said only burdens this novel's lightness, perhaps I can say, before falling silent, that it too partakes of what it describes as "the paradoxical truth that it is only possible for art to assert." That is, "dream with the dreamer, but never forget that the dreamer will wake in a world devoid of dreams."

Not to Fall Silent

Gabriel Josipovici, *Infinity: The Story of a Moment*

Gabriel Josipovici's new novel might be subtitled "the story of a moment," but it is also the story of a man. Avant-garde composer Tancredo Pavone is, says his manservant Massimo, "a singular gentleman," and his singularity saturates this short text. Yet Pavone is absent; we only hear his voice as ventriloquized by Massimo, in an interview after his master's death. So, one voice articulates and amplifies another. The form is familiar, harking back to earlier books by the author – *Moo Pak*, among others – as well as to Thomas Bernhard. And like the best of Bernhard's creations, Pavone is partly inspired by a real person: Italian composer Giacinto Scelsi (1905-88), whose blend of microtonal experimentation and Eastern mysticism Josipovici has characterized as "a curious mixture of profundity and bullshit."

The phrase is instructive, since it signals that Scelsi's avatar isn't to be taken too seriously. Pavone is, like his namesake (the word means "peacock"), a preening creature. And yet, as with *Moo Pak*'s protagonist Jack Toledano, perhaps it is Pavone's bullshit – his all-too-human absurdity – that makes his profundity possible. We shouldn't straightforwardly search for "meaning" in Pavone's tall tales. In *Infinity*, meaning lies less in words than in the rhythm of a voice struggling not to fall silent. And this rhythm is what reveals the voice's frailty, its finitude. As with Reger in Bernhard's *Old Masters*, such a revelation overrides any merely ironic response to the voice or its worldview. So it is with Pavone, who is humanized by a voice which shadows the fact that its speaker is no longer speaking.

As a composer Pavone, like Scelsi, asks "why should the sequence of notes be the essence of music?" Both are opposed to the notion that notes are only "a part of a structure," and Pavone's controversial composition for piano, *Six Sixty-Six*, consists of meditative repetitions of a single note. Unlike, say, Cage, his engagement in such exercises is not intellectual: he is "not interested in the idea" but only "in the sound," where sound is what precedes music; what one encounters at "the heart of the note." For him, "a sound is not a step on the way to something else," as in some strains of serialism. Instead it is, in itself, "a world, an infinite world."

So much for Pavone's aesthetic principles, which permeate *Infinity*'s content. But what if, to paraphrase Walter Pater, the work itself "aspires towards the condition of music," in its form as much as its themes? If the text possesses a structural musicality, perhaps this can best be discerned in its pauses; in those moments when Massimo surfaces from Pavone's soliloquies, interacting with his interviewer:

He was silent.
- Go on, I said.
- Yes sir, he said.
    Since he still seemed disinclined to do so I asked him: did he often speak to you like that?
- Like what, sir?

Here a disorienting slippage between two subjects (where Massimo's "he" merges with his master's) aligns with Pavone's argument that composition is an "art of listening, not of speaking," and that the composer can therefore be seen as a "conduit," not a creator.

Infinity's narrative is a nest of such conduits. Massimo, it seems, is a machine who will not "go on" without prompting, such that the interviewer's requests are akin to a pianist playing notes on a keyboard. And if that makes Massimo the piano, then Pavone's voice is the sound that emerges, in blocks of prose which each comprise a single "note." These passages wander, but they do not "digress" anecdotally. Whereas anecdotes are largely linear, Pavone's voice describes circles, spiraling into itself, returning to its own terms to "transform" them – just as "by playing one note over and over... it is *transformed*." Whenever a note is repeated, each repetition is different. Yet there is also a difference *inside* each note, in which it differs from itself: listen to a sustained note for long enough and you will hear not a note but a sea of modulations. In this sense there is an infinity inside each instant, and *Infinity*'s prose is itself in pursuit of it.

Baudelaire memorably claimed that modern art must combine "the transient, the fleeting," with "the eternal and the immutable." Similarly, in *Infinity* content and form correlate to express an artistic awareness that "eternity and the moment are one and the same." As Pavone puts it, "if you can hear the *now*... you can hear eternity." But if the book is in touch with eternal ideas – lofty beliefs about art and the cosmos – they nonetheless never float free of the work's written form, which gives them their vital embodiment. Every time Massimo rests and then resumes his monologue, all such thoughts are brought back to the voice – indeed, to the voice's bodily basis in "breath," which "all music is made of," and all words as well.

So, *Infinity*'s greatest achievement is that it does not deal in grand analogies between music and writing. Instead it reminds us that both are rooted in raw human material. The book itself is nothing but a breath, a voice, a life, and life only ever lasts for a moment. But even when faced with its finitude, *Infinity* refuses to flee from life, or to try to transcend it. Instead it returns to the life it describes, "plays it again," over and over, so as to transform it. Pavone's life is approached in the way it was lived, in faith to the thought that living life fully might mean finding, or making, infinity inside its limits. When Massimo speaks he may only go on for a moment, but every such moment somehow embodies the whole of a life, which itself was summed up in each of its moments. In this sense, *Infinity* speaks to something in life and art that is simple, familiar, but also miraculous: the feeling that even when something does not last forever, it can last forever.

Between Positivism and Magic

Marek Bieńczyk, *Transparency*

Marek Bieńczyk can be described as a writer without category. He's most well-known as the author of postmodernist fictions like *Terminal* and *Tworki*, although he's not just a novelist. He's also an essayist, a translator (of Cioran and Kundera, among others), an academic literary historian, and even a noted wine critic. True to its author's eclecticism, *Transparency* trespasses between genres: it's neither a novel, nor a scholarly study, nor a personal reflection. Instead it encompasses all of these forms, putting them to work on each other. Fictional passages are framed like the asides of an absentminded academic, and facts are narrated with a novelistic sensibility. Yet *Transparency* doesn't make too much noise about its stylistic modulations; it never overtly announces itself as a new species of writing. Instead it stays in suspension, slipping by almost silently. In this, *Transparency* is not unlike its subject. As Bieńczyk puts it, the book treats transparency "as a theme,"

> as truth and illusion, as the hobby of existence, the graspable handrail against which we may lean our very being, something we might even try to pour into text.

This treatment entails a multifaceted method, partly drawn from the discipline of philology: on one level, *Transparency* is a history of a word, and of that word's relation to a shifting set of concepts. Yet Bieńczyk's is a speculative, poetic philology, a little like that of the Italian philosopher Giambattista Vico. This isn't objective analysis; it's intellectual history in the key of myth. Bieńczyk's concern is with "the connections between transparency and the expressible," from Aristotle (for whom, as he quotes, "there is only transparency," as an underlying reality) to the present, where science has superseded such notions, yet where they're nevertheless necessary, "since the heart of man changes more slowly than the world." An archetypally heartfelt expression comes from Jean-Jacques Rousseau, in whose *Confessions* Bieńczyk discerns a desire for transparent speech; for a clear voice which would make the soul perfectly present to itself:

> Rousseau believed that the heart of man could speak... he saw how language could become a transparent medium for the will of speech, for everything that wishes to be expressed... with no secrets and no depths to be fathomed or understood.

In turn, Rousseau's romantic ideal informed the Enlightenment – "*Lumières* in French," Bieńczyk reflects, "*Aufklarung* in German, all of which say, 'Now we'll see.'" But Bieńczyk goes on to show how such modern ways of seeing have been co-opted by consumer capitalism. From advertising to state surveillance, today's society "obliges us to have a transparent heart," turning transparency into a tool of the status quo, in a reversal of Rousseau's soulful radicalism. Nowadays, as with shop windows, seeing through things is what stops us from seeing beyond them.

The problem of transparency's political value plays out across Bieńczyk's book, whose overall purpose is obscure. One section recounts the history of literary descriptions of glass, detailing "the houses, palaces, domes and arcades packed into the prose of the nineteenth century." In giving voice to this period's spirit of spectacle, does Bieńczyk achieve some sort of authentic articulacy, *à la* Rousseau, or does his writing dovetail with capitalism's culture of "catalogization" and "museification," uncritically aestheticizing the social system? In posing this puzzle, *Transparency* recalls Walter Benjamin's *Arcades Project*, a work which Theodor Adorno famously said stood "at the crossroads between positivism and magic." What Adorno meant was that *Arcades*, a poetic catalogue akin to Bieńczyk's, could on the one hand be read as banally descriptive (positivism), and, on the other, as lulling its readers into blinkered enchantment (magic). *Transparency*, too, must steer between these two poles, to resist being read simply as trifling scholarship, or otherwise as stained glass, as snow globe, as ornament.

Yet Bieńczyk doesn't resolve this dilemma so much as dissolve it. He makes each of its terms transparent, a lens through which we might discover the other. Like Benjamin's, his approach is dialectical. A case in point is provided by a passage on melancholy, itself a major theme of Bieńczyk's oeuvre, and the subject of his earlier essay collection, *On Those Who Never Recover What They've Lost*. "If glassmakers and architects hadn't invented transparency," Bieńczyk muses, "melancholics would have." Yet melancholy, he goes on, is determined by "divergent ways of seeing." The first is that of forlornly staring through a window, a familiar depressive habit, which arouses a sense of "seeing without having... a shimmering collision of sight and frustration." With this we're back in the storefront; the depressive gaze reifies real experience, "crystallizing" and "immobilizing" it, as in an advert. This species of melancholy is, in Adorno's sense, "magical," ornamental. However, there's a second kind of melancholic sight, "the upward gaze," where we cast our eyes away from what pains us, toward heaven. Crucially though, to turn our sight skywards isn't escapism – after all, we'll be brought back to earth once our necks start to ache. But in this "broken, aborted transcendence," we might find a means of renewing ourselves, and of being briefly free of the world, without forgetting it.

Hence, melancholy manifests itself in both passive and active aspects – as a resigned falsification of experience, and as its regeneration. This rubric might be richly applied to a certain melancholic strain in contemporary writing, ranging from W.G.

Sebald to Lars Iyer. But Bieńczyk's literary history touches on another tradition, which unites an assortment of writers under the sign of

> the shared striving for pure light in their texts, their striving for emptiness, for silence... their abandoning of the real, the concrete, the perceptible, the living, in favor of the motionless, the fading, the falling silent.

Such striving can be both formal and thematic – as in Beckett, for instance (whom Bieńczyk doesn't discuss) or Barthes or Blanchot (whom he does). As a theme, it's best represented by the Polish novelist Andrzej Stasiuk, whose books describe "landscapes with minimal human activity." Stasiuk focuses on a world where "life has either not gotten going, or has already been extinguished." Here transparency is, as in Aristotle, "the idea organizing the cosmos" – it sits in the background, the field on which existence occurs. But beyond this, Bieńczyk reminds us, there are writers who treat transparency in terms of textual form. This brings to mind Beckett's letter to Axel Kaun, which likens language to "a veil one has to tear apart in order to get to... the nothingness lying behind it." Bieńczyk's lineage links several figures whose language "flirts with silence," from Chateaubriand to Joubert. In each, he highlights an impulse he calls "negative idealism." Yet this phrase doesn't denote mere nihilism. Like the melancholic upward gaze, transparency here reaches beyond a quiet acceptance of the real. As Bieńczyk avers, "if life has its own utopia, perhaps nothingness does too."

That said, *Transparency*'s charm is that it doesn't try too hard to place itself in such a tradition. In the end, Bieńczyk isn't out to construct a canon, only to follow his thoughts wherever they flow. His book is structured associatively, less like an essay than like our inner experience. Its passages follow no purpose, never leading beyond what's on Bieńczyk's mind. Thus, the trick of

Transparency is that its intellectual content – its roster of knowledge – is in the last instance not intellectual, but psychological. It is what its author happens to know, what matters to him, what he haphazardly remembers. Its narrative isn't an act of assertion, but of introspection and recollection. Kundera described Bieńczyk's second novel, *Tworki*, as "a song that lifts us up and away." The same could be said of *Transparency*; indeed, unlike Kundera's own essays, it has no rhetorical point, and hence no need to marshal the movement of its prose. So much is said in this book, so much pondered and studied, but with a lightness which leaves us unsure whether we only dreamt it. *Transparency* captivates, but is soon blissfully forgotten. People talk about the pleasure of being "immersed" in a book, as if they weren't already immersed enough in everything else. But maybe losing oneself in reading only echoes how one has lost oneself in life. A book should let us look up, leaving life behind for a time, but not leaving us spellbound; not stopping itself from being seen through. Unlike other books, Bieńczyk's *Transparency* both seizes and beautifully frees us, allowing life and literature to become blank pages; to slip into silence.

Truth, Force, Composition

Gordon Lish, *Peru*

"*Peru* is true," insists Gordon Lish in the introduction to this new edition of his masterpiece: "all too grievously true." But empirical truth is irrelevant; the book achieves truth on terms of its own. Whether novels secrete a residual *effet de réel* (Barthes) or deploy the device of a false document (Swift, Defoe) they are defined by their formalization of the *force* of truth; its rhetorical pressure, not its propositional content. As with wish-fulfilment, a book like *Peru* makes a bid to *become* true, in opposition to life, which is anyway worthless. Such a book is a black box, an object at odds with the world around it. *Peru*'s truth lies not in its correspondence to reality, but in its consistency with itself. And this kind of consistency (a quality which Lish has called "consecution") is what allows an artwork to stand alone, asserting its *agōn* against all that is. Art authorizes the impossible, and artistic truths are of the order of miracles.

For this reason, if *Peru* represents a "confession," it is one carried out not in content (confessionalism as a literary genre) but in incantatory form: a performative speech-act addressed to God. The story's specifics therefore matter less than the statement from which they stem: "there is nothing I will not tell you if I can think of it." The thoughts that follow accrue truth through their telling. Gordon, 50, father and husband, catches a news clip of convicts fighting with knives under gunfire from guards. The struggle occurs, he later learns, on the roof of a prison in Peru. Subsequently, rushing his son to a bus bound for summer camp, he is struck on the head by the trunk lid of a taxi. Blunt-force trauma triggers traumatic memory: reeling and bleeding, Gordon recalls how, aged six, he savagely killed an acquaintance while playing in a neighbor's sandbox.

The act is portrayed with an objective coldness, which *Peru's* early reviewers read in terms of narratorial psychopathology. Yet depth psychology is superfluous; personae in books are merely arrangements of surfaces, much like us. *Peru's* apparent brutality results not from some folk-psychological category error, but only from art's overriding imperative to *present* – to "make you see" (Conrad), to "incarnate the abstraction" (Pound on James), or to "characterize... an overall total experience" (Lish in *Peru*). Hence, "you have to imagine dents," declares Gordon, urging us to envisage the murder: "like a trench – in his hair, in his head. Whereas with his face, it was more like a peach pit with some of the peach still left stuck to it." The detail with which Lish describes the damage done to Steven Adinoff's head by Gordon's toy hoe – and even his callous play on Steven's speech imped-iment ("nyou nyidn't nyave nyoo nyill nyee!") - are crucial corol-laries of the book's pledge to tell all that is thought. Consistency of composition is extra-moral, beyond good and evil. In this respect, *Peru* offers proof of Shklovsky's dictum that "art is pitiless." The final sentence of this passage, for instance, provides the sole reason for those that precede it:

> I would have heard it if there had been screams. I heard the water sizzle. I heard the rubber bands. I saw everything – the big white buttons Steven Adinoff had, the blood which got on them, the dents in his hair, the dents which the hoe made in Steven Adinoff's hair, the way the hoe bent Steven Adinoff's hair down into them and how it stayed down there in the dents, got stuck there in them. Nothing is not seen, nothing is not heard.

Violence in *Peru* is compulsively visual – indeed, voyeuristic. Lish's writing reflects a perceptual reflex; the narrative eye reacts as we would to graphic war footage, or to the car crash we want to but can't look away from. When broken bodies open up to perception, injury yields *ostranenie*; the world's deep structure disrupts our sensoria. In this sense, visions of violence can be visionary; ecstatic. From Gordon's perspective, Adinoff appears to *enjoy* his death, as do the prisoners in Peru. Perhaps TV screen and sandbox alike are "evental sites," as per Alain Badiou – states of affairs which transform our access to truth:

> Steven Adinoff knew the deepest thing of all, just like we all would probably prove we do if we suddenly ended up in the same setup as he did with me – plus as those men did with each other in Peru on the roof.

Within the world of the book, the word "Peru" points to a place of primordial wonder and horror, in which killing is innocently consensual, even erotic. Lish localizes this liminal state in the sandbox, which we, eyes held open, are forced to behold. But the physical body is inside the soul, not vice versa; the sandbox itself is merely a memory, mediated by the mystery of infancy. This mystery is the true nucleus of *Peru*, a work which recounts what Nietzsche once called "the seriousness one had as a child at play" – or as Lish has lately put it, "*homo ludens* submitting himself... to the impressive sovereignty of his nature."

Gordon at six is an alien entity, as we all were at that age. His amorphous mind is immersed in magical thinking. His reason for killing his rival arises from "rhyme," and specifically his fantasy that he can "rhyme every word there is" – starting, in the sandbox, with the word "hoe." The results approach religious glossolalia, and are the closest, he claims, "you ever get to feel to the fact that you yourself are God." As an adult, watching two Peruvian prisoners bleed to death by an airduct, he likewise imagines that "maybe one of them in his mind was going like this... *airduct, airduck, airluck, chairlug.*" Here it becomes clear that the concept of rhyme, with its etymological root of "series" or "sequence," is continuous with Lish's credo of "consecution."

And *Peru* implicitly posits this principle – the practice of creation as recursion – not as an arbitrary artistic technique, but as a force of nature. For Lish, *poïesis* is intensely linked to *instinct*, just as it is for his key critical influences, Julia Kristeva and Harold Bloom. As spoken in the sandbox, and by the prisoners on the rooftop, poetic language is derived from a prior grammar of drives, of killing and dying and rising again – it is, as put in *Peru*, "the language of Peru."

Peru itself is structured in strict accordance with this grammar; as always with Lish, a book is an object built up brick by brick. The section titles signal this explicitly: *Peru* is presented not as a novel but as a "property," split into a "cellar" and "roof." The book's building blocks could even be parsed into classes. Firstly, objects, or fetishes: this class would include all humans and animals (there are no "subjects" in *Peru*, apart from the formal subjectivity of the work, which subsumes its contents) as well as recurring keywords such as "hoe," "shoe," "Buick," "gossamer," "rake," "sandbox," and so on. Secondly, sense-impressions: the sound of sprinklers spraying the lawns; the heat of the sidewalk; "the smell of citronella." And then there is the associational logic that yokes these components together. Here, as in psychoanalysis, there is in fact no such thing as "free" association. When the description "wet and pink-looking" prolif-erates across Adinoff's harelip, a girl's genitals (glimpsed during a game of "show me yours"), and a disfigured foot, the chain is tightly constrained by consecution – or what we might call, with Gordon, "rhyme," by which "I don't mean rhymes as we in general mean them. What I mean is like with like."

Linking like with like means weaving a world; so while some readers would regard *Peru*'s narrator as solipsistic, the truth of his situation is that he *is* God. "I was just like God was," Gordon recalls, since "I was the one who had to watch things for people, who had to see things… if I didn't then it wouldn't be." For Lish as for Berkeley and Beckett, *esse est percipi*, and worlds and artworks alike require relentless attention. Gordon again: "when I was six, I thought that I had to keep everything, but everything, in my mind... to keep it all going." These echoes of Beckett become more precise if *Peru* is compared to the latter's late novella, *Ill Seen Ill Said*. In each, a deliberately limited lexical pool provides the "atoms" of a textual world – as it were, the grains of sand in the sandbox. These are then combined and recombined, raked over and over, in a recursive process whereby an artwork *emerges* from chaos into composition. In this way, the work is revealed as a world of its own; one whose language is its limit.

Accordingly, we cannot comprehend Lish's contribution to literature without an awareness that *composition cuts across ontology*, not only aesthetics. For example, Jason Lucarelli has expertly described "consecution" as a writerly toolkit, in his essay "The Consecution of Gordon Lish." But a more complete reconstruction of this concept would call for the following thought: consecution may be less a methodology than a metaphysic; a miraculating agent; an instance of spirit or *pneuma* submerged in the world. In Lucretius, the force of composition is described as a *clinamen* – our world is born from a "swerving" of atoms in their fall from heaven. Such is the purpose served by *Peru*'s perpetual swerving, rhyming and recursion. Each consecutive swerve steps closer toward a total curvature that delimits the work as a world apart. *Peru* is a paradigm of the artwork as a formally closed system. Hence, what has been called "consecution" is not a matter of mere wordplay; it is the way in which such a system defines its horizon.

What lies inside the horizon imposed by a hyperdense work of art? *Peru*'s consecutional poetry draws and then redraws a graph which is populated with more points at each pass. In so doing, it mirrors the temporal structure of traumatic memory – circling back on each of its objects again and again, in an eternal return of the same. This obsessive pressure, which the narrator declares has "turned me looking rearward for keeps," has rightly been likened to Thomas Bernhard's urge to *"go back over everything."* In books by both of these authors, every event that occurs lasts as long as language is in motion: a text could be cut open at any point and disclose the same set of objects and forces; the same composition. But Bernhard's fractal consecution differs from that of Lish, in that the latter exactingly brackets out "culture," at least at the level of external reference.

For my part, I might side with an even more forceful extinction, in which each work of art is newly tasked with eradicating the existing tradition. Consistency overturns history, exposing not a contingent set of experiences, but what Ashbery has called "the experience of experience" – or, as in *Peru's* epigraph, attributed to Agamben, "the memory of memory itself." When such revolutions are reached within works of art, they only endure in the time opened up by the work – briefly, but in that briefness forever. So, in poetry as in *Peru*, "the way you felt when you were six is the way you still feel now… it is always suffocating, the weather is always August."

Literature Is What We Are Lost In

Ivan Vladislavić, *The Loss Library and Other Unfinished Stories*

"These notes deal with unsettled accounts. They concern stories I imagined but could not write, or started to write but could not finish." So begins *The Loss Library*, a collection of unclassifiable texts by South African novelist Ivan Vladislavić. Split into eleven "case studies of failure," the book draws on two decades' worth of its author's "stillborn schemes and incomplete drafts," telling the stories of stories that went untold. Yet every account stands at several unsettled removes from its object. The notes that we read are not Vladislavić's notes toward his unfinished books, nor are they even his notes on those notes. Each essay offers only a reconstituted reflection, an inverse image of an imaginary origin.

In this regard, the project gives rise to a generalizable problem. Its eleven texts clearly "exist," insofar as literature ever exists, but each is predicated on a prior, "nonexistent" model. Are these models therefore brought into existence, achieving a life of their own in the texts that transmit their traces? There's a sense in which an incomplete thing is "completed" if we give an adequate account of its incompleteness. So, are Vladislavić's fragments in fact finished stories?

This paradox is what propels *The Loss Library*. The book doesn't read like something straightforwardly "written." Instead, it is brought into being by the tension between being written and unwritten, where neither ever overwhelms the other. In this way the work doesn't work out, isn't resolved into a work, but rather *results*, inevitably, from a field of forces whose opposed poles are what Vladislavić calls "the beginning and end of story-making."

The first fragment, "The Last Walk," focuses on an image which seems to condense these concerns. Vladislavić recalls how his eyes once alighted on a photograph, now well-known, of Robert Walser lying dead in the snow. Here the death of the author brings about the birth of writing, with Walser's fallen, frozen figure stirring Vladislavić to "write a story about the last days, hours, minutes of a writer." But the story dies on its feet, first dispersing into digressions, then disappearing completely, just as Walser's footprints "break off in mid-sentence," and his collapse "carries him onto the silence of a blank page." Writing is like dying and being born both at once. As Mallarmé wrote to Camille Mauclair, "I only exist on the page; *preferably one that's still blank.*" Like the photograph, then, the scene of writing is static but perfectly preserved: a circular, synchronic world in which, Vladislavić observes, "there is not much else besides snow and the body."

Later essays relate other, more worldly derailments, which any writer might recognize. In "Mrs. B.," the author becomes too closely caught up in his historical research, letting reality get between his words and "the invention of a world." In "Gross," an Oulipian game is simply "abandoned because I lacked the stamina." Some of these texts barely bruise the skin of the invisible books they describe. Yet there are several that seem to cut into an infinite interior. Then, from the inside, we learn that literature itself is "loss," is what we are lost in. Again, a limitless literary space is suggested. In "The Dictionary Birds," Vladislavić envisages an imaginary "aviary," built to house "the menagerie of creatures seen only in the dictionary," those real entities he has only ever encountered in their unreal, readerly forms. But a dictionary bird must be a higher dimensional object than a bird that we see in the sky; life's extent is less than that of literature. Any enclosure for such entities would therefore be endless, or at least, its ends would be imperceptible to us.

Fictive forms preserved in infinite space: the theme achieves its fullest expression in the central text of *The Loss Library*, "The Loss Library." Vladislavić's library is both birthplace and grave, an archive where all unwritten books are assembled and catalogued. The account stands alone as an autonomous story: unlike the other texts in the collection, "The Loss Library" lacks a model. Indeed, it enacts a crucial exception to the rule of the rest of the book: "The Loss Library" is what enables *The Loss Library* to exist. It's logical, too, that the two texts should share the same name, since the story described by "The Loss Library" is also the story of how *The Loss Library* tells its stories. That is, this account of an archive of unwritten books is itself an account of the book in which it is written. The loss library is where all of *The Loss Library*'s incomplete works would end up, with the necessary exclusion of "The Loss Library." What's more, as the librarian notifies the narrator:

> When a reader opens one of these books it has consequences in others. Things are shaken up. Matters that appeared to be settled are reopened for discussion. The extent of the disruption depends on the book. There are certain slim volumes, the reading of which would hardly cause a ripple. And then there are others with the power to change everything. Entire books melt away under the reader's eye, schools of imitators dwindle to nothing, towers of study guides topple over.

The texts in the library are described as "lost" books, but also as "potential" ones. We know by now that these two terms are not mutually exclusive. But nor are books, written or not, isolable from each other. The librarian's warning suggests a systemic connection between them, an intertextuality in which real works are reconfigured by their unreal archetypes. Literature is a holistic structure, more than the sum of its parts. Here that excess is expressed by the endlessness of the library, which we assume is an annex of another "total" library. And any actual book we can hold in our hands is only a point on an infinite line which leads back to that library. Indeed, the loss library could be defined as precisely that place where literature may be perceived in the form of a line, not a point.

Behind any book lies another, unwritten book which itself encompasses every book, whether written or unwritten. All of our books are already "lost," at least insofar as writing a book reduces its unwritten magnitude. In other words, to write a book is to remove it from the loss library. Hence Vladislavić has his librarian advise the narrator that no books may be loaned. To do so would be to collapse a wave function, converting possibilities into fixed instances. But in writing *The Loss Library*, has Vladislavić broken his own rule of silence? To recount an "unsettled account" is surely to settle it, and writing about the unwritten might risk cutting untold stories short. But writing is a double movement. Placing "The Loss Library" inside its namesake posits a place within the work where unfinished works are preserved. So, *The Loss Library* performs its own preservation, re-shelving its unwritten stories by means of the very same motion that makes them appear. Here every removal is a return, every loss a retrieval. Writing uncovers its own underlying condition, but leaves it undamaged, untouched. We arrive at and depart from a scene which remains on display, as if under glass: "the icy death of the author, and the frozen life of the book."

No States, Only the Sky

Dylan Nice, *Other Kinds*

A young man leaves home – a rough, rural town in the
mountains. He reaches a suburban world of relative wealth,
where he meets women who remain remote from him. He can't
adapt, can't go back, can't square where he is with where he's
from. The nine stories in Dylan Nice's debut collection each cut
into the same spectrum of experience, the same essential
estrangement. But although the lives of Nice's narrators are
narrow, they're only as narrow as our own. Unreturned phone
calls, impeded intimacies, homesickness for homes we've
outgrown: surely, for all of us, these fierce longings are familiar.
For me, *Other Kinds* is a book about human finitude. It encompasses not only its narrators' nostalgia and alienation, but also
mine, maybe yours. And in this, the book is borne aloft,
absorbing the bracing scale of the earth – what its author has
called "the size of the world and how it thrills me."

One of Nice's narrators is "a believer in transit," another an
"expert in awayness." All are aware that the distances between
places parallel those between people. "We flew to Los Angeles
without talking," a narrator remarks of himself and his girlfriend
after an argument. "I imagined somewhere below me the Grand
Canyon or the desert and its rock." In these stories, every
landscape is a mental landscape; selfhood itself is spatial. The
relation between place and personality is revealed in another
narrator's self-description:

> I am named after the place I'm from. It's a lot of fog and
> smokestacks. Trailers parked in mud and dog shit. The roads
> circle places you don't want to be.

To be named after a place is to take on its traits. So, smoke, shit, and circling roads speak of this speaker's psychological state, his spirit. Throughout *Other Kinds*, the inside is identified with the outside. In one story, an injured hand is described as "the damaged part of myself." Plainly, this poetic slippage of body and soul is already latent in ordinary language; in our ambiguous uses of personal pronouns. Perhaps such practices are the proper terrain of philosophy. Yet unlike explicitly philosophical literature, Nice's fictions are not fabrications: the mysteries they express are engrained in the detail of real life.

Being alive, embodied, a person in a place, means being both "thrown" and "fallen," as Heidegger has described it. Thrown into the world, we're always falling away from ourselves. We are, writes Heidegger, "homeless." We exist in the distance between where we've been and where we will be: life is delimited by this distance. In the collection's second story, *Thin Enough to Break*, Nice's narrator compares "the great nothingness of God" to "the great everythingness of me." Like us, the characters in *Other Kinds* are ensnared in their low, lonely everythingness. They know the cognitive closure of consciousness can't be escaped. Nonetheless, they long to connect with other kinds of consciousness.

So, intersubjectivity is figured as infinite distance. Furthermore, this distance is gendered. The abyss between human beings is articulated between girls and boys ("I hated that there were boys and there were girls," says the narrator of *We'll Both Feel Better*). Sex is then an unsolvable problem: no one can truly close the space between two separate bodies. "I tried to touch her. I didn't put my hands on her." Later, "he stopped wanting her but kept trying to want her." Such divisions are as much social as sexual: one character is paralyzed because "my people were loggers and truck drivers," whereas "hers hung inspirational sayings on walls." Finally though, the gulf is far more fundamental. "The girl lay there and breathed," we read, "and he knew she wasn't thinking the things he did." Although I can follow another's thoughts, I can't think them. The other always withdraws from thought: I am homeless where he or she is at home. These stories aren't simply about star-crossed lovers, or lovers "from other worlds." In *Other Kinds*, the familiar formula is universalized: for each other, all lovers are star-crossed, or are as far off as stars, as obscure.

Stars are of course surrounded by space, and in Nice's stories space is never negative. Rather, it rushes to the forefront. As with the weather, space rests and then stirs into motion, no longer a ground but a figure, a manifest force. "The wind would be blowing in from the space all around us," notes the narrator of *Wet Leaves*. "I'd put my back to it, arch my brow, and watch her squint and blink against the gusts." In Nice as in no other writer I know, language is alive to vastness: to how the "flatness" of a landscape can "change the shape of the sky," so that we seem to stand "at the spot where the world begins to get round." *Other Kinds* contains expanses so immense they "make motion nearly irrelevant" – environments where there's "nothing on the horizon, nothing in the distance to mark time."

Writing about Plato's *Sophist*, Alain Badiou analyses life in terms of five axioms: "being, motion, stillness, sameness, and the Other." For me at least, the core elements of *Other Kinds* are comparable: a boy, a girl, a place, another place, all separated by space. Close and far, light and dark, wind and sun, warmth and cold: a world. This is why Nice's depictions of movement through space mean much more than they say. Each is, in its way, an epiphany: one of those moments of world-disclosure we know only once or twice in our lives. Every so often, an everyday scene shifts its aspect, pivoting from the prosaic to the essential. In passing, a single perception embodies the whole of human existence:

Big trucks were coming by bright and fast and disappearing

into the flatness. The light at the edge of the sky was orange and thick with twilight. The gusts pulled at my clothes and I could see the men inside, their faces dark while they sat still and drove fast. They found work, driving to some place they didn't know and then back toward the last thing they remembered being good.

Do any of us do anything more? If we don't, might describing the miles between us, the lengths that we go to, uncover what we have in common? In one sense, Nice's stories stage a world before which we can only fall silent. This world is made up of ineffable facts, as one character claims: "things that are true that can't be argued." So, a narrator stands awestruck in front of an ice floe, another before a burning building. And we as readers stand with them, transfixed by suburban streetlights, the smell of rain, clouds in the sky or blood from a cut. Each of these stories swells to a point at which the world simply stills us.

Conversely though, if we listen closely, sometimes the stillness tells other stories. There are two types of epiphany. In the first, the world is illuminated, but only for a lone observer. In the second, the world illuminates who we're with. Although other kinds can't be known, they can be encountered, lit up in lonely silence, like us. As long as this lasts, alone as each other, we know we're no longer alone. In *Wet Leaves*, a quarrelling couple are calmed when the world comes between them – once more, as weather, as falling snow: "the question was quieted by the flakes of snow that began to fall and melt in her hair." White and mute and miraculous, the world sheds light on a person's presence. Suddenly she's beyond all questions: she is the question, the source of a sublime ethical pressure. In *It's Never a Little While*, two interlocutors sit in a pool of light. One tells the other a story, which might be "a lie." His lie, his story, all stories end in the light of whoever sits silently listening. Again, there are truths that can't be argued:

The girl was totally illuminated – what she wanted was so visible her skin seemed to suggest that what she wanted would never go away.

In *Other Kinds*, to contemplate space, the land, the sky, is to confront our homelessness. Vitally though, this confrontation calls us away from solipsism, towards those we share the world with. By the end we're left, like Nice's narrators, uprooted, enraptured, and twice as alive. In the collection's last story, *Flat Land*, a character tries to return to his home in the mountains. He had "left to sort out what was me and what wasn't," but he finds that his home is not as he left it, and neither is he. Leaving again, he is nowhere, no one. However, in this he is open not only to his "everythingness," but to his nothingness, and to everything else beyond it:

The car moved fast in all that space, past the stumps of corn that blinked by in perfect rhythms. I hit the flat land again. It seemed I was part of some big purpose until the size of what was out there exhausted me. Eventually there were no states, there was only the sky that never got any closer and me moving through places I could not stay.

Wide Skies and Wildflowers

Sam Michel, *Strange Cowboy: Lincoln Dahl Turns Five*

Unpublished until now, *Strange Cowboy* was the first novel ever written by Sam Michel, author of 2007's *Big Dogs and Flyboys* and, over twenty years ago, the seminal short story collection *Under the Light*. Michel is married to another innovative author, Noy Holland, and like her, he was taught and initially edited by Gordon Lish. As with many students of Lish, the influence of Michel's mentor looms large over his prose: every sentence in *Strange Cowboy* seems to summon up a new world, tied inside a taut knot of surging, swerving syntax. But beneath Lish's stylistic stamp on this book, one can also discern other voices, more European in origin: Proust's temporal consciousness; the humanist pathos of Joyce; certainly the obsessive discursiveness of Beckett and Bernhard. And *Strange Cowboy*'s story transposes all this into what could be called the true *topos* of modernism – after all, artistic truths are allowed to be counterintuitive – the American West.

In Winnemucca, Nevada, we meet Lincoln Dahl, a faltering first-time father. Like Beckett's Murphy, Dahl sits philosophizing in his favorite chair, transfixed yet transcendent, "unweighted, ecstatic." But his introspection has left him in flight from life, or at least from his wife, his mother, and especially his son. To them he is merely "mothy, paunched, an ineffectual reminiscer." Dahl's son shares his name, as did his dead father, so Dahl is "the middlemost Lincoln," the last male link in the chain of memories that makes his family a family. As such he is duty-bound to become a "model" for Lincoln Jr. His son is a "wheezy, stump-tongued, club-footed creature," nonetheless not unwanted so much as unknown – the child of a parent nonplussed by children. "Deep, deep inside of you," declares Dahl's wife, "way down in your subbest-conscience, I believe you love him." But love can't be brought to life if it is buried too deep to disclose. For this reason, little Lincoln's early years have been swept up in "a woozy spiral of neglect and woundings." Today he turns five, and amid preparations for his party, his mother presses her put-upon husband to tell the story of his own fifth birthday; to relate the reconciling wisdom that "my name, too, was Lincoln... that I, too, was coming up on five once."

"Why should a husband not know what to do?" wonders Dahl. "What could be simpler than to tell a son a story?" And can such a story truly convey a father's tenderness, until now unacknowledged, untold? From such questions, *Strange Cowboy* weaves a lifetime's worth of love and grief, memory and forgetting. Lincoln the elder lingers in his seat for nearly the length of the novel, dreaming of his speech, and in so doing deferring it. His inner monologue telescopes out toward the act it anticipates: time slows down during its refraction through consciousness. As he admits, "tell me a straight line is the shortest way between two points... and I will argue for the scenic route from Happy Hour to Homestead." Casting his mind back to his fifth birthday, Lincoln sets off in search of lost time. But he soon seems as likely to lose himself in time as he is to find it. For him there is "always too much to remember," and thus "the past grows as wide for me as any future; I proceed with no more certitude in recollection than in prediction."

Like the language in which Michel renders it, memory is a dense medium – "the warp through which experience is leavened into weight." In this respect, to remember too much is to risk forgetting oneself; as Lincoln's mother warns him, it is "dangerous to turn the gaze inward." Ever the armchair Descartes, Dahl is the "doubter at the center" of his uncertain reminiscences, "turning through a shrinking future and a growing past and wondering where what went." In this, his inner life is like any of ours: we're all Lincoln Dahl, whenever we're left defeated, dumbfounded, unsure of how we wound up where we are, who we are. If we're regretful, irresolute, living excessively inside ourselves, reflection too easily leads to oblivion. In such circumstances, like Lincoln we will be bewildered by

> squanderings, bygone glimpses into what I meant and did not say, what I said and wished I meant that I were saying, what I felt and could not find it in myself to say that I was feeling.

But is there a means for memory to emerge from this mist; for an act of remembrance to transport Dahl through doubt to faith? If so, might he finally say what he feels and mean it? It takes the death of his son's beloved dog to drag Lincoln from his living room, first to the vet's, then, in a failed bid to find a replacement, to the derelict spot where a dog pound once was. These days the places that populate Lincoln's memory no longer refer to reality: "lamentably, the pound was not a pound," nor can anything lost to the past be properly found. Perhaps, then, the point is not to retreat into memory, but to relate it to the future. Surfacing from his thoughts, Dahl stares at his son: a sad, silent boy, mourning a lost friend, framed by falling snow. Suddenly, somehow, for the first time, Lincoln looks at Lincoln and sees himself.

Read as a road trip, *Strange Cowboy*'s circular journey mimics this movement toward reconnection and recognition. Dahl drives his child to the hospice where his mother lies dying. He collects her, and takes the two of them home with him. Somewhere on the way, he at last starts his story, detailing "a day that was for me the first remembered time through which I could sustain myself," in the hope that it might help sustain his son too. His subsequent homecoming, like Bloom's in *Ulysses*, marks the end of a modest odyssey – one with a subtly self-transformative outcome:

Sure I fetched no living dog, had not managed even to provide a place in which to rest the dead one. Were I my wife, I would see my husband had departed, crossed his distance, and delivered back the same dead dog, a mute son and a husband's mother. Yet here I found another mother, something other than a muted son, here I sounded different to myself, at least. I listened. I was a different kind of quiet... *I must be the difference.*

What Lincoln has learned is that his son has a soul like his own. And by telling his story, he has turned five again too, alongside his child, talking his way away from himself and toward the world he had hidden from; "back to tomorrow," and to "a simpler, unconflicted saying." No longer "meat-pulp in an easy chair, a dreamless self-deceiver," he later tells his sleeping son and mother that he loves them. "From here on out," he decides, "I will dedicate myself to words and deeds of restoration." A lesser Lincoln Dahl might have lived and died without having said what he felt, his mind like so many of ours, "a mailsack stuffed with unsent letters." So for anyone trying and failing to match up meaning and feeling and speaking, *Strange Cowboy*'s tale will ring true. As alive as the West's wide skies and wildflowers, this is a story to see us through the struggle to tell those we love that we love them.

Reservoirs of Silence

Miranda Mellis, *The Spokes*

The Spokes starts with its narrator's arrival in the "afterworld," the land of the dead, although it is not the one her preconceptions of heaven and hell have prepared her for. Instead the hereafter is a holding pattern, a moratorium, where the newly deceased drift around in an aimless "amnesiac hustle," absorbing music and movies, ingesting not lotus flowers but "cold green gelatin." Here Lucia Spoke meets Silver Spoke, her dead mother; a tightrope walker, possible suicide, and "the last performer in the Spokes family line."

> She looked just as I had last seen her, the day of her fall from the high wire... my mother in her Spokes Cirque Rêve costume, as colorful as a summer bird.

Time passes, or perhaps not, as the afterworld is "a realm whose primary substance is not time." Soon Lucia's mother receives a message: "Tell your living to remember." The pair then "possess" Lucia's still-living father, Leo, during an epileptic episode. He drives (or they drive him) to a cemetery, where he fails to find either of their graves, but achieves a broader communion with the "thousands of bones underneath him." Later, Lucia suggests to Silver that they should attempt something similar, conversing not just with their fellow "recent arrivals" but also with the "ancient dead," a vast and unknown population.

So goes the story of *The Spokes*, although simply to call it a "story" would be insufficient. Any text that tells a story also suggests a situation, but *The Spokes* shows a story submerged in its situation, such that a silence washes over it. We see the ship sink, and then, where it was, we witness the waters that bore it. Miranda Mellis's writing is driven not by narrative logic but by magical acts of disclosure, of world-revealing. The syntax of stories is syntagmatic, whereas worlds are holistic; *The Spokes* is both, a story untold in its telling so as to unveil an emergent whole. And for this reason it needs to be read all at once. As with any of Mellis's works, to stop would be to break the spell, severing story from world. To resume after an interruption would be to read another text, just as we can't return to our dreams in the daylight.

From its outset, *The Spokes* is strewn with mythological symbols. Cerberus and Persephone are alluded to in the first few pages, as if to assert that the world of the work is not that of real life. Only somehow it is. In the truth of its experiential tenor this false world makes itself known as our own. Furthermore, such uncertainty can't be safely explained by citing critical concepts – familiar theories of the "fantastic," for instance. Mellis's fictions infringe Tzvetan Todorov's rule that fantastic tales "must oblige the reader to consider the world of the characters as a world of living persons... and to hesitate between a natural or super-natural explanation of events." In this respect *The Spokes* recalls the stories in Mellis's tellingly titled collection *None of This is Real*. There the fantastic is not an eruption in the everyday, a figure which reconfigures the ground of the commonplace. Rather, it is the other way around. Each story is a tissue of unreal events – from mutations to telepathy – into which intrude instances of the ordinary: health insurance; queuing for coffee. Mellis's texts are fantastic tales in reverse, where reality ruptures the field of fiction. Here the real is what estranges and unsettles us; as Lacan would say, the real is the impossible.

Whenever the real appears in a work of art, questions are raised regarding the work's social or political weight. Mellis herself seems to see her stories as responses to "real" problems. The press release for *None of This is Real* refers to "the loss of family, heritage, ecosystems, agency, and power," and the protagonist of the title story speaks of his "political despair." In Mellis's case, perhaps the question of art's political content could be cast as a question of allegory – that is, the kind of question we might ask of writers like Kafka. Indeed, *The Spokes* often evokes the Kafkaesque, with its bureaucratic tone, and its ghosts who await opaque messages regarding "where they were supposed to be and what they were supposed to do once they got there." Moreover, in Mellis's work as in Kafka's, social facts are made manifest as ambiguities: as what one character calls "occult typologies," obscure causes which seem to steer the narrative, yet which never arrive at an explicit meaning. Ultimately, and again as in Kafka, such ambiguities resist allegorical reading, since to specify their sense would be to reduce them back to facts; to strand them in factuality, whereas the truth of such facts is finally found in their fictionalization. If the real world has, as Nietzsche proclaimed, become a "fable," maybe real unfreedom will only be understood when figured as mysticism, as fate.

Thus *The Spokes* transforms its constitutive terms, approaching a transcendent indeterminacy. Within the narrative, the question "what is it like?" is always at issue, and is always eluded, exceeded. To ask what something is like is to cause a story to come into being, but this opening question is also what closes the scope of all stories, what puts a stop to them. *The Spokes* breaks through this logical circle: when Lucia asks Silver, "what was it like between life and death?" her mother replies that "it wasn't really like anything," in the same way that language *qua* "likeness" can't capture her complex motives for falling from the high wire. In short, some stories cannot be told; and *The Spokes* is a story about such stories. In this sense the text attempts to re-enter what it refers to as its "reservoirs of silence." As suggested below, it does so by means of two inextricable themes: memory and family secrets:

The statement *what we cannot speak about we must pass over in silence* had proven useful to us... A family naturally gives up on the insoluble, the unanswerable, the hopeless cases – they are like fossils or mythology. Such subjects are practically Palaeolithic in their indecipherability... For the Spokes, the subject of our silence formed an unacknowledged nucleus around which we orbited with backs turned, looking out at the universe, but never inward. If history brings us all together, secrets dwell on the underside of it, beyond the remedy, reach, and solvency of speech.

Here the Spokes form a wheel whose hub is the secret of Silver's unproven, unspoken suicide. Such secrets exist on history's underside, along with the "thousands of bones" beneath the cemetery, and with the "ancient dead" whom Silver says are "invisible to us, out of time, unrepresentable." But if the after-world stands outside of time, for Lucia it opens onto a deeper "duration." Duration is, as she puts it, "pre-clock-time," an ancestral time in which all far-flung families are reconciled in memory. But it is also the deep time of the story; the silent world which rises within and around it. Frank Kermode once compared fictional time to the *aevum*, the time of angels. The "time-order of novels," he argued, partook of both movement and stillness, temporality and eternity, "like a stick in a river." The same could be said of *The Spokes*, a story which somehow sloughs off time, so as to approach the pure time of fiction. A whirlpool with a whole world at its still, silent center.

Fiction's Reach for Freedom

The Life and Work of Hob Broun

Heywood Orren (or "Hob") Broun (1950–87) published three books in his brief lifetime, none of which are widely known today. But Broun's intense, eccentric fictions ought to be more than a mere footnote to modern American literary history.

His first book, *Odditorium*, could ostensibly be called a "novel," although it digressively destabilizes "character," "story," and almost all other hallmarks of the form. A seedy, pulpy pinball game of botched drug deals and bungling gunplay, the book's pleasure lies in its unpredictability; to read it is to watch it run off the rails.

Broun's next text, *Inner Tube*, was acquired by legendary editor Gordon Lish, whose stylistic influence can be felt throughout Broun's subsequent work. By now Broun had become – a little like Barry Hannah, another author from Lish's stable – a writer less of conventional "sentences" than of freewheeling, aphoristic riffs. But beyond this, *Inner Tube* displays a brilliant strain of misanthropy that is all Broun's own. The book begins with the narrator's mother committing suicide by putting her head through a TV screen. Compelled to escape this constitutive trauma (plus his incestuous lust for his sister), he flees into an increasingly fractured, ersatz social world. Along the way, man is revealed as merely

> an over-evolved creature whose most dangerous enemies come from within... Imagine the first useless panic, the first nightmare, the first crushing turn of *anomie*. Ten thousand generations later, all we can do is palliate. Misery abhors a vacuum, and history is a list of sedatives.

Eventually Broun's narrator escapes from this failed civilization, leaving to live alone in the desert. *Inner Tube*'s plot provides no palliation; instead it presents a pessimistic awareness that "we are animals. All the consoling fabrications must be waived."

Six chapters into writing *Inner Tube*, Broun underwent emergency surgery to remove a tumor surrounding his spine. He lived, but was left paralyzed from the neck down. As he said to his agent at the time, the surgeons had "snipped every God-damn wire." From now on, Broun's very breath was brought about by a respirator. His deep depression during this period is perhaps easy to appreciate. What is remarkable, however, is the way in which he overcame it – willing himself, against all odds, to go on writing.

Broun finished *Inner Tube*, and wrote the stories collected in *Cardinal Numbers*, by means of a mechanical prosthesis: an oral catheter (known as a "sip-and-puff device") connected to a Franklin Ace 2000 computer, running a customized word processer triggered by Broun's breath whenever a letter flashed on the screen.

It's worth remembering how much he resented this set-up: had he "had hands," as he put it, he would rather have written on a 1948 Remington, a picture of which he kept pinned to his wall. Nonetheless, this method suggests a rich metaphor for the role of "technique" in recent American writing. Academics like Mark McGurl have remarked on an implicit "technicity" – a techno-logical turn of the imagination – in the way certain writers conceive of their craft. Ben Marcus, for instance, describes writing as "a delivery-system for feeling," a machine that mediates emotion using rhetorical mechanisms. This terminology is echoed in the title of the course he has recently taught at Columbia: "Technologies of Heartbreak." In a sense, Broun presents an extreme (and, of course, tragically enforced) example of this emphasis on taut, fraught, high-stakes execution.

In Marcus's formulation, the flipside of technique, or

technicity, is raw emotional urgency. And this, above all, is what matters most about Broun. Among more well-known writers, his linguistic maneuvers most closely resemble those of Sam Lipsyte – another author shaped by Lish's painstaking approach to sentence construction. Each writer, in his way, illustrates the Lishian dictum that "every morpheme, every phoneme counts." The point, though, is that such stylistic exactitude mustn't be misread as emotionless. Observing my interest in what could crudely be called the "Lish line" of fiction, an antagonist of mine once claimed that he couldn't see any "angst" beneath the pyrotechnics; any "existential" pressure. Broun's prose provides powerful proof of why this is wrong. Without doubt, here was a writer, as Lipsyte has said of him, for whom "every word was hard won."

Broun's best book by far is his last, the story collection *Cardinal Numbers*. Written in clipped, compressed sentences, these stories share a surface similarity that some might mislabel as "minimalism." But Broun was only a minimalist in the simple, quantitative sense of being able to squeeze nineteen stories into 150 pages. The fact is that *Cardinal Numbers* gleefully runs the gamut of literary forms, from fabulism to free association. The standout story, "Highspeed Linear Main St.," is a shifting, swerving improvisation about modern art and sensory overload. At one point its manic narrator pauses for breath and announces: "modus operandi: montage, collage, bricolage."

As with other books on his list at Knopf, Lish himself wrote the jacket copy for *Cardinal Numbers*. Today, it's hard to imagine any commercially-minded publisher countenancing the ecstatic rant that graces this book's flaps. As is made abundantly clear here, Broun's stories arose from

a tension quite special to those whose lives must be lived in the face of calamitously punishing circumstances. Such condi- tions of existence produced in Hob Broun a living instance of the Beckettian principle *I can't go on; I must go on*, and accordingly made of his fiction a kind of literary embodiment of these opposing statements. To be sure, it is this very irony that suffuses the stories in this book, and that imparts to them the heart-aching air of hope struggling between moments of its being successively suffocated and set aflame. These entries should be read as a map of the will of their author to keep on.

This will is what's behind the lasting value of Broun at his best. Stymied by life, he brought life to his words; the writing of fiction was, he once said, "the focus of what I'm surviving for." To pour all of oneself into writing; this is the challenge his stories set for any would-be author who reads them. And it's why they still stand, decades later, as urgent, ultimately exuberant examples of how writing can address what Lish has called "the problem of being alive." In its audacious inventiveness, *Cardinal Numbers* measures itself against the life its author could not live. Any paralysis, it seems to say, can be briefly escaped in feats of verbal velocity; in fiction's reach for freedom.

The papers record that Hob Broun died in 1987, accidentally asphyxiated when his respirator broke down. He was 37 years old. "Ice Water," the opening story of *Cardinal Numbers*, was recently reprinted in *New York Tyrant*, one of America's leading literary magazines. At the time of his death, Broun had begun work on a third novel, reportedly called *Wild Coast, Wild Coast*, which, to our loss, no one will ever read.

Start from Zero and Count Backwards

Kjersti Skomsvold, *The Faster I Walk, the Smaller I Am*

Kjersti Skomsvold's first novel was born while its author was bedridden, convalescing after an illness. She started putting scraps of prose on post-it notes, and over four years she wrote and rewrote, until she had finished *The Faster I Walk, the Smaller I Am*. This brief text is completely unified, and nothing of its early notational life survives in its structure. But its roots in its writer's experience of enforced isolation are evident everywhere. The book seals up a single concern, making it an airtight container for one perfectly encircled emotion: loneliness.

Mathea Martinsen lives alone, an elderly widow, her links to the world loosened by something that seems like social anxiety or dementia. The book imagines her last monologue, echoing, perhaps, Beckett's *Happy Days*. Her late husband, Neils (or as she calls him, "Epsilon") remains absently present, his afterimage imprinted on almost every phrase of her narrative. At first we're uncertain whether he's physically with her or not; her consciousness flows between memory and present perception so seamlessly that each resembles the other. It isn't simply that Epsilon's ghost lives on in the grain of her voice. Her voice itself is a single surface: although its curvature conjures up illusory entities, deep down it knows nothing of individuals. On this level, Mathea's inner life is liquid; her mind is like the sea.

In a sense, Skomsvold's book is nothing but a voice – a voice whose horizons coincide with those of a mind. And in its intransitivity, this voice could be said to find its bedrock in what Deleuze called "the univocity of being." Or as Mathea terms the world's indivisible whole, "totality." Her problem is that she feels estranged from this totality, yet yearns to return to it.

"Perhaps I should stop seeing myself as an individual and start identifying myself with the totality," she thinks, "but... I'm about as far away from it as you can get." Skomsvold doesn't need to explain her character's sense of estrangement, because the limits of the book are those of Mathea's mind. After all, no one ever really knows why they are the way they are.

On one hand, Mathea longs to lose herself in a benignly entropic universe, obeying her mind's inward pull toward dissolution and death. But an opposite impulse calls her to cling to her life's specificity, searching for any attributes that make her unique – bathetically put, at one point, as a matter of "what my name is, or what my favorite color is, or which cassette tape I'd take with me to a desert island if I could choose only one." To be sure, Skomsvold makes much of Mathea's personal quirks, and thus we could claim that her voice is caught, or pulled taut, between the totality and her own personality.

Importantly, there was a point in her past when these axes converged. As a young girl she was struck twice by lightning on the same spot. This lightning strike stands at the apex of her life's arc, as trauma and miracle. The event cemented her identity (until then "nothing had ever singled me out") and at the same time it almost erased her altogether. In other words, it was at once a point of origin and a vanishing point. The incident also introduced her to Neils, whose first words to her were, "the chances of being struck by lightning twice in the same spot are less than ε, if ε equals a microscopically small quantity." So she named him Epsilon, and they eventually married.

Her later life can be seen as an effort to recapture this moment, both as individuation and oblivion. Her search for the former takes the form of "trying to leave some traces behind," whether by burying a time capsule in her backyard, or just observing the bite marks her crooked teeth leave in her food. As a child she used to count stones in the playground, and her adult attempts at self-definition echo the pleasurable autism of children's games.

Arranging pebbles to spell her name in the sand, she remarks on the merit of "giving meaning to meaningless things." Her actions recall those of Beckett's Molloy, stashing stones in his pockets. This may make playing with pebbles look like a sign of inner impoverishment, but Mathea's small joys are genuine. In the same way, whenever she says "what's the point?" the question's not framed in depressive rhetoric. It's more like the innocent "why is there something rather than nothing?" asked by children, and by philosophers.

Achieving uniqueness poses problems for Mathea, who's so sensitive that she's unsettled by the multiple entries for "Mathea Martinsen" in the phonebook. Meaning to ascertain which one's real, she tries to call her own number, but the line's busy. Analysts from Lacan to Laing have claimed that self-formation somehow splits the self, and that isolation leads to psychic involution. Mathea's phone call metaphorizes this process: any act of positing a self for herself prevents her from accessing it. A similar crisis occurs when she composes a note to put in her time capsule: "I write, 'I alone am Mathea.' When I look at what I've written, I see 'I Mathea am alone.'" Here her drive to define herself is what entails her solitude. Moreover, whatever sense of self she secures will always be "less than ε," now that she has lost Epsilon. This is why her thoughts so often start from zero and count backwards, as when she thinks "before Epsilon, my heart was like a grape, and now it's like a raisin." The uniqueness she seeks is infinitesimal.

Any ageing life must give in to oblivion, so what's the point in being unique? After all, reasons Mathea, "every person in China is just as unique as me," and, in the end, as alone. Since this is so, isn't the best way to live to become "more and more exposed to death," inching away from oneself and towards what one isn't? Mathea remembers how "in our wedding picture... I'm not easy to see because the background was the same color as my dress." If to be is to be perceived, and life isn't life if it goes unnoticed, what wins out in Skomsvold's story is a dying woman's drift into the invisible. Yet Mathea doesn't suffer death passively, as a tragedy. The final sentences of *The Faster I Walk, the Smaller I Am* aren't sad, or aren't only sad; they're also euphoric. Mathea's dying moments are "dark and clear." When she was younger, she unintentionally left her dog to drown in the sea. "The possibility of that happening," said her husband at the time, "must be less than ε, if ε equals a microscopically small quantity." But when she swims into nothingness, she's no longer alone. She swims out to be with them both.

The Far Side of Fiction

Gerald Murnane, *Barley Patch*

Gerald Murnane's *Barley Patch* begins *before* itself; in a sense, it begins before literature. Like all books before it, the book is brought into being by a question. "Must I write?" asks Murnane's narrator, a man we might confuse with the author Murnane, but who is nonetheless not him, since *Barley Patch* is, in its own words, "a work of fiction." The book is the opposite of an autobiography: instead of issuing from its author, it entails or "implies" him. Not only this, but it implies that all books imply their authors, in the way its own is implied. As such, *Barley Patch*'s implications appear to touch on a "pure" form of fiction.

The implied author of *Barley Patch*, a novelist named Gerald Murnane, reports that "in the early autumn of 1991... I gave up writing fiction." His opening question, "must I write?" then gives rise to a related one: "why had I written?" The rest of the book is conjured out of these questions, which we might regard as atomic models of the kinds of questions that cause all stories to be told. Much of the book is built out of memories, brought together in an associative chain stretching back to the author's childhood. Each memory calls to mind another memory, and every description suggests second-order descriptions that can't be described. The book's subject, says Murnane, consists of "what I call for convenience patterns of images, in a place that I call for convenience my mind, wherever it may lie or whatever else it may be a part of." A sentence like this deserves to be dealt with carefully. The author's mind, in this case, lies partly within the work of fiction; he has admitted his own fictionality. Where then can what he calls his "network of images" come from?

A clue is provided by *Barley Patch*'s break with the rhetoric of authorial "imagination." This much misused word, Murnane reflects, "seems to me connected with antiquated systems of psychology... with drawings of the human brain." In refusing itself recourse to this language, *Barley Patch* retreats beyond reach of romanticism; the book is hallucinatory, but in a way that differs in kind from, say, De Quincey. Yet it also abandons the prearranged reading paths of realist novels, presenting instead a series of scenes set for stories that forget to occur; it progresses by means of digression and detour. So where does it go, now that it can no longer return to the mind of the "real" Murnane?

Murnane the narrator, the one with whom we resolve our route through the book, remarks that "a work of fiction is not necessarily enclosed in the mind of its author, but extends on its farther sides into a little-known territory." This territory radiates out from the work, taking in the types of experience that envelop it, and that enable our access to it. After all, any work is always partly porous, blurred on both sides by the reading and writing minds it implies. And what is implied both is and is not "inside" the work, which is not an object of absolute sanctity, but one which at once includes and is impacted by its being written and read. In this way, we could conceive of the work as coming together within what Hans-Georg Gadamer describes as a "fusion of horizons," available via the overlapping encounters that we call reading and writing. Thus, the answer to each of the questions above would be that the work resides in, is brought about by, and is itself a transitional space that those who engage with it enter into.

The space that spreads around and beyond *Barley Patch* is populated by "personages." A personage, explains Murnane, is not a "character" so much as a kind of character-in-waiting. In one sense, what comes before any character is the "image" that guides its construction; a glint in the mind's eye of the writer. But such images are, again, transitional, "made up" just as much by the reader. Reading another author's story, Murnane recalls how he found himself "assigning to the female character... a face that

I first saw during the 1990s," which is indeed how reading seems to work. A writer cannot fix a face to a character; characters are not completable, which means that other entities will always be glimpsed through their gaps. And if these echoes and ghosts predate crafted characters, they can't be pinned down to one point of origin; they emerge from what the work opens onto. It's said that researchers in the field of face recognition rely on "eigenfaces," phantasmatic figures derived from the vector space that contains all possible human faces. A "personage" in Murnane's sense is somewhat similar; a point on a map of the place that precedes characters, and that makes them possible.

This ontology, in which the "origin" of the work evades any vanishing point, is itself figured within *Barley Patch* by means of a memorized image. The image in question is Claude Lorrain's *Landscape with Samuel Anointing David*, the "painted backdrop" to the stage at the Capitol Theatre, where a young Murnane and his schoolmates once took part in a concert. Like when Murnane says of his early reading habits that he "moved among the characters," so, as a child, he dreamt of inhabiting the place that this painting depicted. But Lorrain's landscape doesn't merely manifest a set of fictional entities. Instead the painting's pattern of light implies what Wittgenstein would call a "change of aspect." As Murnane makes out, it isn't the scene's foreground but its background that has somehow become "the most brightly lit of the visible zones," suggesting that what lies beyond may be "more richly illumined still." Thus,

> I saw myself as travelling from the shadowy foreground into the brightly lit distance, past the bridge and the river and then across the grassy countryside. For a few moments, I would have seen the illustration as other than a patch of painted scenery hanging in a shabby room in the place that I called the world. I would have understood that what I had taken for distant background was brightly lit foreground. The persons

around the veranda were of little account. Anyone peering in on them from the darkness behind them mattered even less. I would seem to travel to the end of the grassy countryside, while the light around me intensified, and while I strained to make out the first details of the land that began where the painted places ended.

Wherever art appears to end it begins again; every horizon it reaches reveals a new one. On this level, then, Lorrain's landscape discloses a diagram of an open, ongoing origin. In the same way, Murnane claims, even when literature seems to lead back to "life" (as when the author of *Barley Patch* tries and fails to tell the story of his conception) it can't help but lead to a literature beyond literature. Indeed, every text written or read implies another that lies in the distance, and whatever setting a writer describes suggests to the reader "a further region never yet written about." Behind the book, a place made of blank pages: "a country on the far side of fiction."

To attempt to locate this country would be to pursue an illusion. Still, such a pursuit might not be meaningless; it may be all that can be accomplished. One clue as to how to characterize this aspect of art is provided by Michael Wood, in his critical study *Literature and the Taste of Knowledge*. What, asks Wood, might a novel be said to "know" that its writer and readers don't? Indeed, what might it know without itself knowing it?

What *Barley Patch* knows is that, in its words, "a work of fiction is capable of devising a territory more extensive and more detailed by far than the work itself." It would be easy to infer from this that a work's boundlessness amounts to its "essence." But Murnane means something more important, which we can relate to works by most writers. Let's say that a "literary device" is, more often than not, one which makes use of what Wood calls a work's "knowledge." In that case, literary language is language that touches upon the tacit dimensions within the work. That is, language is "literary" whenever it interacts with its implicature. Enrique Vila-Matas, for example, says of a story by Hemingway that "the most important part does not appear in the text: the secret story of the tale is constructed out of the unsaid, out of implication and allusion." Of course, Beckett also called the work of art "complete with missing parts."

If this is true, to assert that literary works open up "other countries" is not to make a metaphysical claim, but to call attention to the way the content of a work exceeds whatever words are read or written. Paul Ricoeur once suggested that when we encounter a work we do not reach "inside" it, as if to recover some isolable core. Rather, "the ensemble of references opened up by the text" results in a "world" which "unfolds" in front of us. This may be so, but *Barley Patch* also knows that works and their worlds always unfold away from what is said and known: that literature is found within its own withdrawal.

No Rings, No Bouquets

Gary Lutz, *Divorcer*

Early on in Gary Lutz's latest book, a nameless narrator makes a typically "Lutzian" observation about the trickiness of linking language to lived experience; the difficulty of literary description:

> You can't generalize about divorce, and you can't get too specific about it, either. The subject either clouds up or loves itself too much.

Perhaps it's not too much of a push to read this remark as "representing" what arises after it. If so, it would seem to set up *Divorcer*'s seven short fictions as attempts to express a traumatic event ("divorce") in terms that retain some faith to its distressing resistance to utterance. When we talk about trauma, our words are quick to thicken over what we want to say. What is more, for Lutz, an ordinary word like "divorce" never cleanly or healthily means what we think it means. If these pieces possess, more than Lutz's others, a collective sense of *intentionality*, an "aboutness," that doesn't mean that they're simply, solely "about" couples uncoupling. Instead, they're better read as documents of a deeper procedure of separation; what we could call an "emotional complex," albeit one that Lutz never lets float free of its textual enactments. *Divorcer* is the work of a technician, not a romantic.

So, it's as if divorce has seeped into the structure of these "stories," like a rot in the grain of their language; something sweetly corrupt that can't be cut out of them. It's buried deep in their syntax, motivating the phrasing that estranges the opening of any errant sentence from its end. In each of the book's seven entries, words are put to work on pulling something apart – a family, a body, a memory of bodies together – in ways that render how life's breaking points really feel when reached. Shards of language are arranged into snapshots of how things have become, as Lutz puts it, painfully "halved."

Another way of saying this is that the book begins to articulate something like a *grammar* of divorce, or maybe even a mathematics of it. In this sense, it soon becomes clear that divorce has something to do with *difference*, the unbridgeable gulf that alienates two separated states or entities. As Lutz's narrator says,

> I'm sorry, but they had a different way of talking about subtraction back when I was in school. It wasn't "Take this away from that;" it was never a matter of *minus*. It was "Find the difference of." E.g., "Find the difference of 54 and 31." So go ahead. Find the difference of her and me.

Finding the difference becomes a recurrent figure for the book's "operationalizing" of divorce. In the third entry, "Fathering," a son is sent home from school bearing two drawings of an everyday domestic scene, "identical except for six things... could he find all six?" When only five are found the problem prolongs itself, taking on a tone that's half-farce, half-nightmare. Father and son resort to ever more desperate measures together, straining their eyes to tease out the remaining discrepancy. In the end, it's the wife who provides the solution that captures divorce at its abstract core:

> In the one on the left, it looks like the phone is just about to ring. But why should I always be the one calling?

"Fathering" describes what a sociologist would call the "disembedding" of a nuclear family; the way it can end up excavated, emptied out across an alien context. Here the family's separation, or self-differentiation, takes place along several vectors: schooling and adultery are the two most obvious, but both branch off into fractal patterns; ever subtler gestures of estrangement. What matters most is that family and society seem to be structured by grammar, in the same way that sentences are. Divorce cuts through life and language alike, all at once, and at the same angle.

Another tool for slicing up what one of Lutz's anti-characters calls "that baleful preposition *with*" is to split a human body into fetishized sites, or partial objects. The intention here is to leave a person "suddenly *pieced*, unseeable as a heinous human whole." Indeed, the bodily whole is habitually shunned by Lutz's skulking narrators, who wheedle out ways of distracting us from it by focusing in on its less wholesome elements: a stray pubic hair; a scar; uneven teeth; a cheap tattoo. In this way a body is broken up, divorced from itself, parceled into discrete morphemic units. A related technique involves the withholding of people's names, in favor of a finicky detailing of those names' phonetic properties (one is "richly hyphenous"; another "broke itself out of the alphabet... queered the mouth that pronounced it"). Here we enter the territory that Lutz has made so notably his own: the severance of a word or phrase from what we thought we knew of its semantics. Readers looking for Lutz's now familiar brand of defamiliarization will not be disappointed by *Divorcer*, which yields, among other arresting examples, the following:

> *Couple...* had for ages also meant "not necessarily two but a quantity constituting more than one and as many as a few."
>
> *Mrs.*, pronounced *misses*, to be construed as the conjugation meaning *suffers the absence of.*
>
> She had taken "brush with death" to mean "apply death smoothly and gently to your life."
>
> If I say that we had sex, all I mean is that we possessed it one at a time while the other of us had to make do without.

It is said, isn't it, that you "make" love because it's otherwise not really there?

For theory-inclined critics, there's a readymade rhetoric for making sense of what a book like *Divorcer* wants from its words. Roland Barthes writes, in *A Lover's Discourse*, about "touching" language as if it were a "skin," a fleshed out, eroticized surface with "words instead of fingers, or fingers at the tip of words." But Lutz's language makes such theories seem naively utopian. In Lutz, if something's pressed against the nerves of a word, you can be sure it's pursuing a more questionable pleasure: a wayward taste or touch. These words aren't served up for Epicurean textual enjoyment. They're there to be interfered with; not so much savored as guiltily binged and purged.

At one point, the narrator of "Womanesque" complains that words and feelings are forever being "fished out" of themselves, or else unearthed from each other. I remember reading a news story once about mismade children's toys that turned out to be stuffed full of needles. This is more like what happens to words in Lutz; something perverse or unnerving gets conjured out of their innards, and doesn't stop coming. Soon enough you can't move for it.

If *Divorcer*'s divorces suggest a generalized grammar, they may also add up to something like a mythology, or a symbology, of divorce. Each entry is threaded through with the same few archetypal moments: a lost lover packing his or her reclaimed belongings; the filing of taxes; the return of wedding presents "by the cheapest of mail." Some stories sketch out uneasy ceremonies; there are, needless to say, "no rings, no bouquets." Another repeated pattern sees the parting partner's personal effects, their wreckage, arranged and rearranged in their remembrance. The narrator of "The Driving Dress," a husband who diets to fit into his second ex-wife's clothes, notes that *divorce* is not the opposite of *marriage*, but of *wedding*: "what comes after divorce isn't more and more of the divorce." But something in the guts of Lutz's book implies otherwise: some redistributive urge that can't help but go on ceaselessly sorting husbands from wives, wives from husbands, dressing each up as what's left of the other. Understood in these terms, even the merest reshufflings are shot through with degrees of divorce:

> To be sure, my wife left me those three times as practice, as exercise, and once in a demure, evermore sort of way that didn't stick, and there was the time we went our separate ways but in intimate parallel, shoulder to shoulder and still under the same roof, and the time she put her things in storage by picking up each thing in the room where it lay and then setting it down again in the very same place, but with the understanding that it was merely stashed away there now, in holding for some later date.

For all that, *Divorcer* is a book that deserves to be read with delicacy, and I can't say for sure whether anything I've said should really be said of it. I want to say more, but can't, or shouldn't, about the book's sorrow – about the frail beauty of bodies badly lived in, of lives intolerably embodied, and of words that sadly fail to span the gaps they're spun across. It should be enough to say that every sentence briefly brings something true to new expression: some black shape moving underwater.

Sweet Emptiness

Andrzej Stasiuk, *Dukla*

I won't say anything about Andrzej Stasiuk, and I'll try not to say much about myself. About Poland, I'll say nothing. This text doesn't need to be contextualized. Equally though, *Dukla* shouldn't be subjected to a "close" reading. Perhaps the words on the page aren't worth as much as we think. What matters is the way that a work *presents* itself. The experience it evokes; the constellation of images it conveys.

This is not simply something linguistic. Literary language is not what makes literature literature. I could subtract all literary devices from *Dukla*, or paraphrase it in purely prosaic terms, and it would still be *Dukla*. Books aren't what we as readers believe them to be. There's something beneath the words that we read. With *Dukla*, one way of saying this is that language is "backlit." The book is lit up by something shining behind it.

Dukla should not be read critically, only impressionistically. It should be read while in bed, the book becoming a bridge between being awake and asleep. It shouldn't be concentrated on, still less interpreted. It's a book to be read with the eyes while the mind is kept empty.

Dukla is a small town close to the Carpathian Mountains. *Dukla* is a discontinuous set of descriptions of Dukla. Because the book bears the name of the place, the two seem to stand in some sort of relation. Perhaps the relation of *Dukla* to Dukla approaches an axiomatic model of what links a work to its object. But if so it's a doubled relation, since reality is already relational. Stasiuk's subject is not so much Dukla as what Dukla reflects or refracts: what its reality relates to him. He doesn't just look at a landscape; in so doing he looks through a lens at what makes a landscape possible. The aim is to train the eye on the root of every relation: *light*.

So, this is a book that wants to look at the sun, although it can't do so directly. As Stasiuk says, "light can't be described, all that can be done is to keep imagining it afresh." Light may be made obliquely available to literature, but only through multiple layers of mediation. *Dukla*'s particular formula for filtering light is to focus it through a memory of a perception of a place. Literature as viewing apparatus; language as camera eye. At one point, Stasiuk reflects on his reason for writing this way:

> I always wanted to write a book about light. I never could find anything else more reminiscent of eternity. I never was able to imagine things that don't exist. That always seemed a waste of time to me. Events and objects either come to an end, or perish, or collapse under their own weight, and if I observe them and describe them it's only because they refract the brightness, shape it, and give it a form that we're capable of comprehending.

Is light then the same thing as God? No. It's merely "reminiscent" of eternity, homologous with it, or situated in a similar structural position. Nothing would exist without light, because nothing would *appear*. Elsewhere Stasiuk implies that light is *causa sui* and will outlive the cosmos. But unlike God, it isn't transcendent. *Dukla* takes pains to deflate false claims to transcendence, theological or otherwise. Its mysticism is more akin to that of Wittgenstein, who once wrote: "everything is as it is, and everything happens as it does happen."

There's a scene, therefore, where Stasiuk berates his grandfather's Catholic faith; his devotion to the "utterly nonexistent." Later we learn that "the soul is a fiction of the mind," a weak counterweight to the world of phenomena. Wherever we turn, the book seeks to stop "transcendence getting in the way of immanence." But this doesn't mean that *Dukla* isn't religious. It is richly religious, yet its entire religion is contained in two phrases: "that was how it looked," and "that was how it was." This concretization also yields an ethics, where what is good is what "has no desire to be more than it actually is."

Light illuminates everything real. At the same time, it annihilates anything not. When a novel channels light like a prism, whatever isn't *essentially* novelistic is stripped from it. This could easily encompass everything we think we know about novels. And such knowledge is precisely what we should suspend when we read *Dukla*.

The first thing to be purged from the book is its plot. "There'll be no plot," says Stasiuk, because plot "melts away in the rising light of day." Instead there'll be "nothing but events," arranged on a flat field where nothing takes narrative precedence: "nothing of any importance is going to happen, nothing." *Dukla*'s beauty is essential because it's all surface, all the way down. No subtext, just text. No depth, no metaphysics. Instead, scenes from a life are simply shown. In the end there is no novel, and all that's left is what is sensed and felt.

Writers often ask how a work made of words might acquire the force of an image. For my part, preferring grace over gravity, I wonder how a book could live up to the depthlessness of a dream, or the weightlessness of the cinema. Sometimes I feel like if heaven exists, it will be empty, sun-bleached, blissfully superficial. Stasiuk's art is one of, in his words, "tranquil annihilation." In *Dukla* a series of scenes simply appears, while never being "set." In this way, perhaps words should accomplish no more than a "pointing towards," a *deixis*. A book should just take the shape of what happens.

For these reasons, to read *Dukla* is to be denied the humanist delusion that the novel you're reading is "about" you; that it speaks to your experience. But beneath this it captures some other, more common commonality. The most common ground is one that's completely depopulated; emptied of every contingency. In Heidegger's sense, a space has to be "cleared." As Stasiuk puts it:

> This must have been what the world looked like just before it was set in motion: everything was ready, objects poised on the threshold of their destinies... the landscape, unpeopled to its furthest limits, looked like a stage set on which something was going to take place only later, or else already had.

Light will also wipe out any "narrative voice," that illusory presence that novelists posit, always perched on the verge of vanishing. "One day I cut my finger," Stasiuk recalls, "and what came out was transparent like the sap of a plant." In *Dukla* the very consciousness of the novel is returned to this state of transparency; we *see through* the novel's narrator, as we see through an optical element. "It's exactly as if I were an extraneous addition to the world... all that comes into my mind are events, nothing more."

To me it seems like dreams are driven by a similar logic. In a dream I encounter myself, not as myself, but as an unfilled function of what happens. In dreams I feel as others see me; an object without an interior. I exist for as long as some "story" is told. I exist because it is told, and for no other reason. My dreams are as close as I come to being fictional. The art historian Joseph Koerner, standing in front of one of Friedrich's *rückenfiguren*, remarks that

> I do not stand at the threshold where the scene opens up, but at the point of exclusion, where the world stands complete without me.

In *Dukla* the world, as well, is no more than a momentary "obstacle to the passage of light." Indeed, every entity, every person or object (the book doesn't distinguish between the two) is "made of the same thing as everything else," and will one day, soon, revert to a single substance. Thus, a ruined building on the road to Kežmarok "slowly turns into something mineral," just as every other physical thing erodes and grows "indistinct, imprecise." Entropy will level life out into a serenely "indifferent" monism, in the same way that *Dukla* restores literature to an indifferent innocence.

For all that, *Dukla* is not, after Flaubert, a "book about nothing." Such modernist moves belonged to the last days of literature, whereas *Dukla* reunites literature with its prehistory. It is not that nothing happens in the world, but that the novel must eradicate itself if it is to capture what happens. Fiction threads itself over the real "the way cotton candy is wound around a wooden stick," but once it's finished "there's only a sweet emptiness." What is a novel worth, anyway? Next to a film, a photograph? Precious little, unless it's no longer a novel, more a "magic lantern, a camera obscura, a crystal ball." In the same movement in which *Dukla* destroys the novel, it comes close to uncovering its inner light. What is erased is retrieved as unwritten.

On Theory

Theory's Renewal

Terry Eagleton, *The Event of Literature*

"Literary theory," Gerald Graff has remarked, "is what is generated when some aspect of literature... ceases to be a given and becomes a question to be argued in a generalized way." Graff's definition might look like a platitude, but, in a sense, its prosaicness is its strength. It's surely the case, as Graff implies, that any systematic account of literature is always and already "theoretical." If so, perhaps theory should be understood less as a phase in the history of criticism – as in the so-called "theory boom" of the 1970s and 80s – than simply as part of the grammar of critical practice. The assumption, today, that theory is "dead" thus speaks not of the failure of some theoretical "project," but only of critics' failures to reflect on their own ongoing theoreticism.

Terry Eagleton's career has covered the long arc of literary theory's fortune, from its institutional incorporation – a paradigm shift partly brought about by his bestselling textbook, *Literary Theory* – to its subsequent forgetting; its false overcoming. As he puts it, "semiotics, post-structuralism," and so on are now "for the most part foreign languages to students." What has taken their place is a kind of uncritical *culturalism*; "a shift from discourse to culture," which often renders the object of study all too diffuse. An adjustment of focus from literary to cultural "texts" may make the discipline seem more inclusive, yet it risks losing sight of what should surely be the crucial question of criticism: what is literature as such?

So, to treat literary criticism as a subfield of cultural studies is to miss the specificity of literary experience. Against this trend, Eagleton's latest book, *The Event of Literature*, attempts to retrieve some of literature's strangeness and singularity. Indeed, it argues that critics should again (as they did in the decades of "high theory") explicitly situate this singularity among their key concerns. In this respect, Eagleton makes a persuasive case for returning to what could be called "pure" literary theory; a pursuit which would stress such apparently overlooked questions as "what is fiction," or "what do all works of literature have in common?" To theorize in this sense is to reassert the centrality of close literary analysis, recovering literature as a determinate object of study, distinct from broader conceptions of "culture." For Eagleton, culture doesn't go all the way down.

Historically however, literary criticism has always had to look outside itself for its own renewal and legitimation. Eagleton's new approach is no exception: he quickly finds that the fundamental characteristics of literature – what he calls its "fictional, moral, linguistic, non-pragmatic and normative" qualities – have received far more comprehensive treatment from philosophers than from literary critics. In particular, he appeals to analytic aesthetics, arguing that this field "contrasts favorably with the intellectual looseness" of mainstream literary theory. Insofar as the latter is marked by a "continental" bias, and by a consequent one-sidedness about literature's philosophical import, the move is a bold one. Indeed, Eagleton's best attribute is his refusal to come down on either side of the unnecessary divide between "theory" and analytic philosophy.

Literary Theory was notable for its deflationary tone; it never naively enthused about the ideas it explored. *The Event of Literature* possesses similar strengths. For example, Eagleton convincingly questions the assumption (a commonplace among theorists since Jauss and Shklovsky) that literary language accomplishes a revolutionary defamiliarization of our routinized existence. As he argues, much theoretical rhetoric in this vein "takes it as read that common-or-garden norms and perceptions are impoverished, and that dominant conceptual systems... are bound to be restrictive." This is, he declares, "a banal sort of dogma," since "not every margin is healthy, nor every system diseased." Throughout the book, he refutes such conceptual simplifications, returning literature to the "rough ground" of reality.

Yet if the exaggerated radicalism of theorists comes under scrutiny, so too do the trivialities of philosophers. For instance, Peter Lamarque is lambasted for his circular account of literary value. As Eagleton summarizes, this approach reduces "valuable literary works" to "those which prove responsive to the normative reading strategies of the established literary institution." On this model, then, "a literary work, like an affectionate pet, is one which responds positively to a certain way of being handled." This institutionalist tendency is not only tautologous; it inevitably tilts interpretation towards positive evaluation. For Lamarque, that a literary work "is rewarding" is a precondition of its being counted as literature. His philosophy thus leaves no room for a truly critical engagement with literary texts. It places evaluation prior to interpretation, resulting in a conservative kind of belles-lettrism.

The Event of Literature covers an ambitious amount of ground, and as a result its arguments are frequently framed in generalities. As in his other recent books, Eagleton's broad brush strokes are both a strength and a weakness. They're a strength in that they enable him to uncover the commonalities (what he calls, with Wittgenstein, "family resemblances") between a diverse set of thinkers and theorists. But, here as elsewhere, Eagleton has a weakness for straw men. One such would be Paul de Man, of whom he announces, "for this Nietzschean theorist the world itself is a linguistic construct" – to which one might answer: no it isn't, and nor is it for Nietzsche. At his most glib, Eagleton isn't as funny as he thinks he is: "if the theorists are open-neck-shirted, the philosophers of literature rarely appear without a tie," runs one dreary routine. A more serious shortcoming is that his rhetoric of robust "common sense," which deploys everyday

counterexamples against the confusions of theorists and philosophers alike, often only holds up at this anecdotal level. In such
cases, when Eagleton ranges competing ideas against each other,
it's pretty clear that he's the one pulling the puppet strings.

Indeed, Eagleton spends slightly too much time demolishing
others' arguments, or dubious representations thereof, and too
little developing his own contribution to literary theory, which is
largely confined to his last chapter. This is all the more unfor-
tunate, since his approach is a reasonably rich and promising
one. It revolves around a reassessment of literary works not as
straightforward reflections of the real world, nor as autonomous
artefacts, but as pragmatic strategies; as projects which seek to
solve problems. Hence, literature tries to contain reality's contradictions, while at the same time reproducing them, in such a way
that each work is an ongoing (indeed, interminable) "event." As
Eagleton argues, "the literary work conjures up the context to
which it is a reaction," in the process "throwing up problems,
which it seeks to resolve, creating more problems." The idea
suggests a productive unpicking of ingrained distinctions
between the form and content of literary works, between their
performative and constative aspects, and even between their
interior and exterior. Yet as it's presented in *The Event of
Literature*, it doesn't feel like much more than a sketch. A longer,
less diffuse account would be required to turn it into a fully-
fledged literary theory. In this sense, Eagleton may have mapped
a route towards theory's renewal, yet it will remain for others to
follow it.

The Prism of Literature

Franco Moretti, *Distant Reading* and *The Bourgeois*

Although he has been writing since the early 1980s, the Italian literary scholar Franco Moretti has recently risen to prominence for his provocative importation of quantitative methods –"graphs, maps, trees," to cite the title of one of his books – into the supposedly "soft" academic field of comparative literature. Initially trained in the Italian Marxist tradition of Galvano Della Volpe and Lucio Colletti, Moretti later moved on to make inventive use of evolutionary models of literary history. From there, he adapted Immanuel Wallerstein's sociological "world-systems theory" into a method for mapping literature's global geography. But it is as the founding director of the Stanford Literary Lab – a center which, since 2010, has conducted "literary research of a digital and quantitative nature" – that he may yet make his most ambitious mark on the discipline.

Moretti's new collection of essays, *Distant Reading*, provides a retrospective of his remarkable trajectory. Reprinting classic papers from the last two decades – landmarks include "The Slaughterhouse of Literature" and "Style, inc." – the book reconstructs the development of what must be Moretti's most controversial concept: the titular idea of "distant" as opposed to "close" reading. This principle first appears in an essay Moretti wrote in 2000, "Conjectures on World Literature." Here he laments the entrenched narrowness of almost all literary criticism – its restriction to reading one "great book" after another, rather than reaching for literature's wider entirety:

> The trouble with close reading (in all of its incarnations, from the new criticism to deconstruction) is that it necessarily

depends on an extremely small canon. At bottom, it's a theological exercise – very solemn treatment of very few texts taken very seriously – whereas what we really need is a little pact with the devil: we know how to read texts, now let's learn how *not* to read them. Distance is a condition of knowledge.

For all its theatricality (Moretti mentions in his preface that it was "partly meant as a joke") this provocation contains a serious insight into the limits of practical criticism: the point is that closeness too quickly conflates *reading* with *knowing*. For Moretti however, literary texts on their own aren't legitimate objects of knowledge – and nor, by extension, are critically sanctified canons. Instead, critics should take the whole of literature as their object, and literature in this sense isn't a "sum of individual cases" but a "collective system," which calls for correspondingly systematic methods. Moreover, Moretti aligns his proposed paradigm with technological progress. As he argues, the rise of electronic corpora such as Google Books (or indeed Stanford's own "Lit Lab Corpus," which "includes about 3,500 nineteenth-century novels") promises unprecedented access to literature in its totality, graspable through the aggregation of what we now call "big data."

One of Moretti's most striking performances of "distant reading" is 2009's "Style, inc." Here he makes a dramatic perspectival leap, taking statistical snapshots of "7,000 titles of British novels, from 1740 to 1850." This approach, he claims, breaks down the constraints of traditional critical models; outdated modes of close reading, against which he hopes to "read the entire volume of the literary past." Even so, Moretti's methods also purport to produce new knowledge of specific texts – as in the case of his later paper, "Network Theory, Plot Analysis," which diagrams the connections between characters in *Hamlet*. Thus, for instance, a visualization of characters' roles as "nodes" in a network reveals Horatio's hitherto unremarked centrality to the play.

Of course, many readers might object to Moretti's reductionism – or, more precisely, his "scientism." Yet the specter of science isn't exactly new to literary studies. As the sociologist Michèle Lamont has observed, "interpretive" disciplines such as English have often strategically sought scientific cachet. From I.A. Richards to Vladimir Propp, the history of criticism has partly been about the pursuit of scientific rigor, such as might stabilize the subjective uncertainties of critical reading. Moretti, too, for all his projected originality, recapitulates this search for legitimation; hence his revolution belongs to a longstanding lineage. And the very successiveness of these bids for validity signals that they never fully succeed: if criticism is a science, it is one that can't be perfected.

In this regard, some of *Distant Reading*'s most interesting moments come when an experiment slips astray from its scientific ideal. In fairness Moretti, like any good scientist, freely flags up these failings himself – whether ruefully confessing a lapse into individual taste ("I like Balzac better than Dickens, forgive me") or regretting an undesired "drift from quantification to the qualitative." The question, however, is whether such "drifts" can ever be corrected. What if, contrarily, literature *is* this drift, these errors and excesses that are engrained in our reading experience? Indeed, if we could correlate every text in existence, surely we might still end up missing literature's essence. As critics, we must always consider the likelihood that literature isn't the *kind* of object our methods momentarily make it. In any case, critical distance can be complemented by critical closeness – an interplay that Moretti acknowledges in discussing his other new book, *The Bourgeois:*

> The fact that *Distant Reading* is publishing alongside *The Bourgeois* – a book that couldn't be more unlike it in spirit and

execution – makes me think that I prefer studying tides and moon independently of each other. Whether or not a synthesis will follow, remains to be seen.

Moving from the moon to the tides, as it were, *The Bourgeois* deals less with the brave new world of big data than it does with a lost world: that of a "vanished" social class and its culture. For Moretti, there is something "ghostly" about the nineteenth-century bourgeoisie – once the essential "embodiment" of capitalism; now its obsolete cast-off. He examines this extinct species by excavating the "fossil remains" of its foremost literary record: the realist novel, a genre which György Lukács once called "bourgeois epic." In fact, Moretti's method in this book is as indebted to Lukács as to the laboratory. Like his Hungarian predecessor, he sees the true traces of social relations in literature's *form*, not its content – as he asserts, "I found the bourgeois more in styles than in stories." And although his stylistic analyses here draw on corpora, as per *Distant Reading*, their textural attention to "the buried dimension of language" owes as much to a more old-fashioned approach: the commendably "close" cultural philology of an Erich Auerbach, or a Raymond Williams.

So, Moretti sets out to study "the bourgeois, refracted through the prism of literature." What this means is that he moves between social history and narrative structure, searching for "the fit between cultural forms and class realities: how a word like "comfort" outlines the contours of bourgeois consumption," or "how the tempo of storytelling adjusts itself to the new regularity of existence." Characteristically, he has little to say about characterization, or, for that matter, plot – such abstractions presumably belonging more to the lay psychology than the "science" of literature. Moretti is much more concerned with the concrete behavior of words on the page; with, say, "the oblique semantics of Victorian adjectives," or "the role of the gerund in *Robinson Crusoe*." In his hands, however, this apparently arid approach proves so revealing that it partly bears out the bold claim, "the past speaks to us *only* through the medium of form."

The set-piece of *The Bourgeois* is a brilliant analysis of syntactical patterns in Daniel Defoe. Moretti reads *Robinson Crusoe* – "the great classic of bourgeois literature" – as a grammatical manifestation of the worldview that Max Weber called *Zweckrational*, or "instrumental rationality." For Weber, this sensibility – roughly, a way of seeing the world not as an end in itself, but as a means to an end – was vital to the rise of the "capitalist spirit." Moretti shows how *Robinson Crusoe*'s linguistic constructions incarnate this spirit, rendering "instrumental reason as a *practice of language*." Throughout the novel, Robinson's narration repeatedly passes from the past gerund (for instance, "*having stowed* my boat") through the past tense ("I *went* on shore") to a final infinitive ("*to look* about me.") This tripartite structure treats each action in a sentence as "the stepping stone for *more* action, and more beyond that," opening onto a future which is itself open to further instrumentalization. Unlike earlier literary forms – the epic or the romance – bourgeois style eschews transcendent meaning in favor of labor: a rational accumulation of worldly rewards. This, then, is the "style of the useful," the work ethic transposed into prose.

Subsequent sections flesh out this theory of prose's stylistic attunement to the "tonality of bourgeois existence." Focusing his linguistic lens on Flaubert and Austen, Moretti discovers a proliferation of so-called "fillers" – descriptions of everyday non-events that serve no pivotal narrative purpose. Thus, in *Pride and Prejudice*, "people talk, play cards, read a letter, drink tea," to such an extent that there is a sense of "the background conquering the foreground." Moretti sees this as the stylistic sign of a *rationalized* existence; fillers fulfil a social logic which limits life's meaning to its minutiae:

Rationalization begins in the economy but spills over into the sphere of aesthetics. Fillers rationalize the novelistic universe, turning it into a world of few surprises, fewer adventures, and no miracles. They are a great bourgeois invention, not because they bring into the novel trade, or industry, or other bourgeois "realities" but because through them the logic of rationalization pervades *the very rhythm of the novel*.

In this respect, then, the book's basic premise is simple: literature's rhythms reflect those of life. As Moretti puts it, prose secretes a "style, in the broadest sense: a way of *being* in the world, not just representing it." This is an important point in itself. But it is also important for its implications, which perhaps put the best parts of *The Bourgeois* beyond the scope of scientific "distance." The idea of life's implication in literature is an old one – recalling, of course, F.R. Leavis. And if ways of being are grounded in grammar, Wittgenstein also looms into view: "to imagine a language is to imagine a form of life." Consequently, we might question Moretti: can forms of life be fully disclosed at a distance?

The life that inheres in literature seems too capacious to be captured by a particular critical method. Ironically, many of Moretti's methods rely on instrumental reason – his ideal of distance belongs to the bourgeois spirit. But criticism can't be contained by what any one critic wants of it. Indeed, criticism reveals rhythms of its own, and these are not necessarily those of science. Critics – like Moretti – might make loud proclamations of progress, or of radical paradigm shifts. But beneath the clamor, when we listen closely, the rhythm sounds rather more cyclical, more self-renewing. Even if science and society advance in a linear style, criticism cannot. All it can do is circle around literature, and, in this, around life. And perhaps all its problems and promises arise inside this circle's description – one which never stops.

Outside the Oulipo

Daniel Levin Becker, *Many Subtle Channels: In Praise of Potential Literature*

For over fifty years now, the (mostly) French phenomenon known as the Oulipo (short for *Ouvroir de Littérature Potentielle*, or "Workshop for Potential Literature") has been baffling and enthralling readers everywhere with its array of opaque literary techniques. Founded in 1960 as a subcommittee of the even more enigmatic Collège de 'Pataphysique, the group has included such luminaries as Italo Calvino, Georges Perec, and Raymond Queneau. The latter coined a phrase that has caught on as a précis of what Oulipian writers do: they are, Queneau claimed, "rats who must build the labyrinth from which they propose to escape." In other words, such writers work within self-imposed "constraints," submission to which encourages their creativity.

Put simply, the Oulipo is partly about puzzles. From palindromes to lipograms and other linguistic devices, Oulipian texts are crafted with what one member calls "the finest sort of needlework." A well-known example would be Perec's novel *La disparition*, written without the letter "e." Here I'll come clean: I don't always see the appeal of these games. From what I've read of the Oulipo's output, I'm a bit ambivalent. A case in point would be Perec's masterpiece, *Life: A User's Manual*. I first read this book completely naively, unaware that its plot was modelled on a sequence of chess moves mapped by a mathematician. I enjoyed it immensely. But as soon as I knew how it had come about, it lost its allure. I couldn't read it without being reminded of what seemed like an annoying authorial trick, a self-congratulatory gimmick. Of course, the fault was entirely mine; my reading of Perec was weighed down by my own presuppositions about how literary works should behave. But it's worth being clear, when it comes to the Oulipo, that I'm neither an expert nor necessarily a believer.

Fortunately, Daniel Levin Becker is both. This young American writer has been a member of the Oulipo since 2009. Moving to Paris on a scholarship after college, he was enlisted by the group as an *esclave* (literally "slave") and commenced an apprenticeship organizing its official archive, the *fonds Oulipo*. Before long he was invited to join. His book clearly benefits from his scholarly work with the group's "paper trail" – its meeting minutes, correspondence, and other obscure apocrypha. More than this, it benefits from his insider's perspective, meaning not merely his membership, but his vivid way of conveying his lived experience of the group. *Many Subtle Channels* is a book about the Oulipo, but it's also about what the Oulipo means to its author. It's a personal appraisal.

In trying to understand the Oulipo, the first problem one faces (if trying to understand it isn't already a problem) is how to grasp the group as a collective entity. Becker's descriptions are by turns deflationary and elevated: in his hands the Oulipo is first "a sort of literary supper club" and then "a hallowed echo chamber for investigations of poetic form and narrative constraint and the mathematics of wordplay." What he's getting at is that it's somehow *both*. Indeed, he subtly captures his subject's capacity to be silly and inconsequential and, at the same time, scientifically serious. Put simply, the Oulipo is serious without being *self*-serious. Becker traces this tendency back to the group's early years, when 'pataphysical pranksterism got mixed up with the mathematical methods of the "Bourbaki" collective. The result was a characteristic cocktail of rigor and irreverence.

Does it make sense, then, to call this conceptually slippery affair a "movement"? The question is complicated by the Oulipo's own attempts to accrue all the hallmarks of one; the trappings, if not the internal coherence. For instance, it has actively fabricated a history for itself, focusing on what co-founder François Le Lionnais called "anticipatory plagiarists" – pre-Oulipian prototypes from Lewis Carroll to Gottfried Leibniz. Added to this, the group asserts its identity not just in its acts, but also in an obsessive inventorying of those acts. The Oulipo comes out of Becker's account looking like a distinctly bureaucratic organization. Actually, that's not right. Rather, it's a performative parody of bureaucracy.

Of course, this is something it shares with many avant-garde movements (like Tom McCarthy's "International Necronautical Society," to take one of today's examples). It also shares an ethos of imitativeness: as Becker notes, "a reliable indicator" of a technique's Oulipian merit "is whether or not it inspires riffing from other members." Importantly though, unlike most modernist movements (especially its key precursor, Surrealism) the Oulipo is avowedly unprogrammatic. Becker again: "it is concerned with literature in the conditional mood, not the imperative… it does not purport to tell anyone what literature should or must be." In this respect, maybe it's less like a movement and more like what some members believe it to be: "an unwritten, collective, and necessarily unfinishable novel" starring its authors as characters.

The Oulipo's main contribution to literary history is its central concept of "constraint," which lets writing arise out of paradoxically productive rules and restrictions. One consequence of constraints is that they free writers from a romantic ideal of spontaneous creativity. Becker quotes Gilbert Sorrentino on this: "constraints destroy the much-cherished myth of 'inspiration,' and its idiot brother, 'writer's block.'" Indeed, Becker argues, the Oulipo was "designed to discredit" writers' and readers' fondness for a false impression of literature as a matter of "ecstatic intuition." The latter sounds suspiciously like what I was disappointed to see disappear in Perec, once I knew what his rules were. Maybe I wasn't ready to have my romanticism demystified.

But this discrediting of aesthetic dogma does seem full of fertile possibilities. One of Becker's many striking character sketches deals with Jacques Jouet, of whom the Oulipo scholar Warren Motte once said, "he writes to pass the time." Becker's Jouet appears engaged in a near-revolutionary conflation of art and everyday life. Sat on a train composing his "metro poems" (one line per stop, and transcribed only when in a station) he breaks the barrier between inspiration and what has to be one of modernity's most uninspiring routines. In this way, Becker says, he "extends the range of potentially potential activities," making life itself as anti-utilitarian as the best art. Again, this is very much an avant-garde staple: life as art, as unprincipled play. In this sense there's something almost Situationist about Jouet, and perhaps about aspects of the Oulipo.

Yet Jouet's poetic method is only *suggestive* of a Situationist politics. The Oulipo has signally failed to follow such political tendencies to the end of the line. On this score, Becker cites the Canadian experimental poet Christian Bök, who claims that Oulipian constraints are themselves constrained to producing "solutions to aesthetic, rather than political problems." The *potential* which Oulipians exercise is essentially apolitical. One critic Becker doesn't mention is the Cambridge academic Alex Houen. For Houen, the whole idea of literary "potential" is freighted with revolutionary resonances. He regards potency as utopian, a force aimed at making things possible. For this reason his rich study of the subject, *Powers of Possibility*, totally excludes the Oulipo, and rightly so. Yet Becker reminds us that, after all, Perec and co never attempted to gild their work with political pretensions: "these were never the terms that the Oulipo set for itself." To be sure, it's admirable that the group has avoided "the pitfalls of the party line." But perhaps Oulipian practice is problematic insofar as it's only interested in writerly, readerly, purely procedural revolutions.

There's a tension, too, between this autotelic aspect of the Oulipo and the accessibility that Becker asks of it. He would like, he asserts near the end of the book, "to make these ideas belong to everyone, not just littérateurs." For him an Oulipian approach is as applicable to life as it is to letters. Removed from the hermetic realms of reading and writing, an Oulipian mindset might "give us the tools" to unpick the aesthetic patterns embedded in everyday existence, renewing the cognitive novelty of "newspaper clippings and restaurant menus and radio traffic news."

Psychologically, such acts of pattern recognition also speak to a search for security. Becker suggests as much, when he concludes that under all its conundrums the Oulipo's essence is the "less sturdy but more human" archetype of the "Quest." On this model, to live your life like an Oulipian is to "move through it with the purpose and security that come from knowing you hold the tools to give it shape and meaning." This is an uplifting thought, although it risks being read as narcissistic: an annexation of the Oulipo's energy to a kind of West Coast existentialism, where "potential" would be reduced to self-affirmation and self-fashioning. If we're to learn life lessons from literary practices, why not make them less individualistic, more politically committed? But in any case, Becker's heart is in the right place. His personal perspective is compelling, and his book is beautifully written. So wonderfully written, in fact, that it's entirely worth reading even if, like me, you remain unconvinced by the Oulipo, an outsider looking in.

Utopic Impurity

Tom Eyers, *Post-Rationalism: Psychoanalysis,*
Epistemology, and Marxism in Post-War France

The recent reappraisal of the French theoretical journal *Cahiers pour l'Analyse* (1966–69) marks a major advance in our understanding of the history of continental philosophy. It also provides a unique opportunity for sharpening our sense of the conceptual makeup of that tradition, whose nuances are too often obscured by a mythology of crude, tectonic clashes: the opposition of structuralism to phenomenology, for instance; not to mention the constitutive distinction between the "continental" and the "analytic." It could be argued that such schematisms belong in part to the genre of what Joel Isaac has called "epic history" – that is, a history that portrays knowledge production predominantly in terms of dramatic divisions and paradigm shifts, while overlooking the subtler connections and continuities that characterize the process of thought in the making.

Indeed, thought in the making is precisely what the *Cahiers* represent. Founded by students of Louis Althusser in 1966, the journal styled itself as a "laboratory of concepts," a test site for new intellectual assemblages. Its experiments were embedded in a complex combination of Althusserian Marxism and Lacanian psychoanalysis, guided by a notably "analytic" commitment to conceptual rigor and logical formalization (figures such as Frege and Cantor numbered among its touchstones). In most intellectual histories of French philosophy, the *Cahiers* have been eclipsed, slightly misleadingly, by the likes of *Tel Quel* and *Les Temps Modernes*. But it was within these pages that many now famous thinkers negotiated their philosophical self-formation: the journal's often remarkably young contributors included the likes of Alain Badiou, Jacques-Alain Miller, Luce Irigaray, and

Jacques Derrida.

Tom Eyers' book is one of the first to take the *Cahiers* as its corpus. In this respect it complements *Concept and Form* – the two-volume collection published by Verso – as part of a broader project of assembling and assessing this neglected material. However, Eyers sets out his own specific thesis concerning the philosophical moment embodied by the *Cahiers* – a moment which, as he puts it, articulates "the highest, seemingly most abstract point of what has come to be known as French structuralism." For Eyers, the question of just what structuralism *was* has been too hastily answered. In contrast, his argument complicates the received reasoning that defines structuralism primarily as a diffusion of Saussurean linguistics, or as a reaction against the existentialism of the 50s. Such partial accounts, argues Eyers, "have frequently served to sever the crucial link between 'structuralist' thinkers and their predecessors in the philosophy of science."

Consequently, this book contends that "structuralism" – at least, the archetypical "high" structuralism documented by the *Cahiers* – can be fruitfully redescribed as what Eyers calls "post-rationalism." As he demonstrates in great detail, this iteration of structuralism was constructed in continuous dialogue with earlier epistemologies – in particular, the philosophies of science elaborated by Gaston Bachelard and Georges Canguilhem. Such philosophies are prototypically "post-rationalist" insofar as they "simultaneously affirm and transcend their basis in Cartesian rationalism," emphasizing both a rationalist commitment to formalization, and, at the same time, an awareness of the "constitutive impurity" of the objects and subjects of knowledge, in their instability and interdependence. This rich, non-monolithic remodeling of rationalism was what "made possible the anti-empiricist, anti-positivist materialism of the *Cahiers* innovators." And in retrospect, a renewed appreciation of this tradition might even serve to subvert today's prevailing assumption that philosophy must be beholden to "either a scientistic empiricism on the one hand, or an irresponsible relativism on the other." The lesson we learn throughout Eyers' book is that thought is always more finely grained than such forced choices lead us to believe.

The bulk of the book consists of close, careful readings of key texts from the *Cahiers*, including such landmarks as Miller's "Suture" and Badiou's "Mark and Lack." What emerges from these readings is a sophisticated sense of the "theoretical friction" at work within the supposedly stable structuralist edifice. Overall, Eyers aims to unsettle several misrepresentative myths. Even a cursory account of the intellectual project of the *Cahiers* would be enough to cast doubt on the familiar caricature of continental philosophy as an irrational current of thought, opposed to principles of objectivity and verification. But Eyers' excavation takes a further turn: within the apparently airtight rationality of high structuralism, he reveals a distinctively post-rationalist dynamism; a "founding impurity" that "goes all the way down." As he asserts,

> I reject what has, at least in some readings, been imputed to French theory prior to the emergence of deconstruction: a rigid metaphorics of structure that is impervious to the dynamic incursion of the new... one of the aims of this book is to underline the dynamization of structure that post-rationalist authors performed.

So, against this assumption of static, synchronic "rigidity," Eyers shows us a structuralism always and already in internal tension with itself – "torn," from the outset, "between the permanence of structure and the necessary contingency of the subject." According to a common conception of the progression from high structuralism to its "post-," the former represented an "arid formalism," too exhaustively deterministic to allow for any account of dynamism and change; of structural transformation and disruption. Close attention to the *Cahiers* proves particularly instructive in discrediting this narrative; as Eyers explains, the journal's young contributors were driven by a desire to discover the fissures and flaws within the structures they explored – the paradoxical (or, to adopt Miller's terminology, "utopic") points which would leave those structures prone to "instability and interruption." Thus, the post-rationalist project can be defined in terms of its attention to the *dynamic* dimensions of structure; "the ways in which the conditions for the emergence of structure are always and simultaneously the potential conditions for their dissolution."

In this respect, Eyers' rubric of "post-rationalism" clears the ground for a new, more nuanced conception of structuralist thought – a structuralism rigorously observant of the crosscurrents between such ostensible oppositions as subject and structure, concept and object. Moreover, Eyers reconstructs this "recognition of the constitutivity of impurity" at the level of a *common* logic – a set of homologies or family resemblances that shed fresh light on the "logical moves" made by a range of post-rationalist thinkers, from Bachelard to Derrida. Indeed, the real strength of the book lies in the lucidity and robustness with which it carries out this valuable project of conceptual extraction and reconnection. Not only this, but Eyers extrapolates further insights from the logic of post-rationalism, which help to subvert certain contemporary orthodoxies. For example, his comparative reading of Canguilhem and Deleuze destabilizes the still-common schema that separates French philosophy into two strands: on the one hand, philosophies of the concept; and on the other, those of life. Eyers' research is therefore of far more than merely "historical" import; rather, it serves the exemplary purpose of rendering even our present logics productively "impure."

Nonetheless, perhaps Eyers' exclusive attention to "the precisely *theoretical* makeup" of structuralist theory necessarily risks neglecting the *ends* of such theory. After all, if the contributors to the *Cahiers* sought to pinpoint the "impurity" of logical structures, they did so, in large part, for political purposes – however abstracted or displaced. As Peter Hallward points out in his introduction to the first volume of *Concept and Form*, the *Cahiers* arose in response to a particular post-war political conjuncture in which "it was no longer plausible... to present social or economic structure as effect rather than cause." In this context, the journal should be read in relation to its explicitly politicized predecessor the *Cahiers Marxistes-Léninistes* (1964–68), and therefore, as Hallward puts it, to "the more general Althusserian project of a *formation théorétique*," a theoretical training "that would secure the science of historical materialism." In short, each of these journals conceived of conceptual work as, first and foremost, a mechanism for authorizing political practice.

Of course, it is important to emphasize that Eyers' project is itself admirably – if only implicitly – political, insofar as it seeks to recover, from the *Cahiers*, an alternative to the reigning forms of knowledge production under contemporary capitalism. But it could be argued that the contemporary import of Eyers' findings cannot be fully articulated at the level of conceptual logic alone. In this regard, it is surely the case that conceptual reconstruction would have to be complemented by a greater degree of historical contextualization. Now, this is not to say that Eyers' project suffers from some sort of contextual deficit that should be redressed – this would be to seriously misunderstand its scope and its stated intent. Instead, it is only to suggest that the revaluation of high structuralism as "post-rationalism" could constitute a key component of a more extensive enterprise, in which Eyers' richly descriptive – or rather, redescriptive – account of the "precisely theoretical" would be matched by a far more forcefully normative account of the precisely political. In this sense it could be said that Eyers has restored, with

remarkable clarity and comprehensiveness, the crucial details of
a bigger picture – one whose continuing reconstruction will
further accentuate its political resonance, past and present.

Significant Insignificance

Ben Kafka, *The Demon of Writing: Powers and Failures of Paperwork*

"The true locus of significance," Roland Barthes once remarked, "is insignificance." In this compelling book, media theorist Ben Kafka claims paperwork as a site of precisely such significant insignificance. From book-keeping to form-filling to filing, most people see paperwork as something that gets in the way of proper work, or that has to be arranged around it. But for Kafka, paperwork functions as figure, not ground: *The Demon of Writing* demonstrates how clerical labor has crucially shaped politics and society since the eighteenth century.

The book begins by defining paperwork as "all of those documents produced in response to a demand – real or imagined – by the state." This initial description signals Kafka's preoccupations: his project blends political history with the more "imaginary" realm of psychoanalysis. Hence, borrowing from Judith Butler's *The Psychic Life of Power*, he specifies his subject as the "psychic life of paperwork," meaning the ways in which the medium merges the inner world of the unconscious with the outer one of imposed social control. On this model, paperwork intersects as much with our innermost desires as with the workings of government.

As a case in point, Kafka cites the story of French civil servant Edme-Etienne Morizot, who in 1788 unjustly lost his job at the Ministry of Finance – and later, it seems, lost his mind. Petitioning the National Assembly for compensation, Morizot became embattled and embittered by bureaucratic requests for "supporting documents." As a result, he proved as prone as we are today to "the fantasy that an omnipotent but benevolent authority will intervene," and thus that the state might magically "satisfy" the desires of its subjects. To begin with, Morizot just wanted his job back. But by the end "this basic need had transformed itself into a complicated demand for recognition by the new state." So, Morizot's plight put paperwork center stage, at the scene of the citizen's psychic investment in a shifting political sphere, "a world of privilege becoming a world of rights."

In this respect, the French Revolution could be considered to have heralded a "new ethos of paperwork," which Kafka portrays as the procedural foundation of the modern state. But such foundations are often far from stable – consider the infamous "dimpled chads" of 2000's Florida voting ballots, for instance. Be it misread, mislaid, "overdue or underdone," paperwork is profoundly unpredictable. And in this sense the state, like us, has historically been "both founded and confounded by its encounters with paperwork."

As proof of paperwork's volatility, Kafka recounts a rich assortment of bureaucratic blunders, tracing what happens when official procedures fail or foster unforeseen outcomes. In 1794, towards the end of the Terror, the actors and actresses of the Comédie-Française were saved from summary execution when the very files that had authorized their accusation abruptly vanished. They owed their lives to one Charles-Hippolyte Labussière, a lowly clerk who had smuggled their papers into the baths, soaked them until they were "almost paste, and then launched them, in small pellets, through the window into the river."

Labussière's lesson, Kafka construes, is that while on the one hand "paperwork syncopates the state's rhythms," every so often it inadvertently "destabilizes its structures." In other words, if paperwork is a condition of possibility for state power, it is one which sometimes paradoxically renders such power impossible. In Labussière's case, the files that facilitated the functioning of the security state were what revealed its vulnerability: from then on, "not only was power resistible; it was water soluble."

This sort of instability was soon intuited by Saint-Just, who said of the proliferation of paperwork during the early days of the First Republic that "the demon of writing is waging war against us: we are unable to govern." His remark reveals paperwork's place at the crossroads between what sociologists would call "structure and agency." Administration may be the medium through which a government's edicts are exercised, but, by its nature, it also engenders new opportunities for escape. Paperwork is "refractive," argues Kafka: "power and knowledge inevitably change their speed and shape when they enter it." When they do, they produce the prospect of their own opposition.

The Demon of Writing delivers a witty and rich history of the faltering rise of bureaucracy since the French Revolution. But beyond its many amusing anecdotes, it also makes a polemical point. Kafka's stories of clerical error cleverly show how theories of the state should more closely consider our everyday experiences of its "failure." And as most people will appreciate, paperwork provides a perfect point of departure for such an analysis.

Of course, Kafka is not the only scholar to have taken a "technical turn" in recent times: Bruno Latour has explored legal theory's embodiment in files and dossiers, for example. While such work speaks of a worthy commitment to the study of material practices, Kafka could be said to have gone one step better. His point is that paperwork necessitates not only a theory of practice, but one of what Freud called *parapraxis*: of unconscious slips and shocking upshots. Whether we're powerful or powerless, the practical world is one into which we project our impractical needs, and where "we never get what we want." In pinpointing this, Kafka's book brings unpredictability back into the picture. And it does so with a panache that makes us appreciate our most "insignificant" acts anew.

Terror and Beauty

Martin Hägglund, *Dying for Time: Proust, Woolf, Nabokov*

The Swedish philosopher and literary scholar Martin Hägglund has swiftly established himself at the center of some of today's most lively intellectual debates. Since the publication of his pioneering book *Radical Atheism*, Hägglund has played a pivotal role in the ongoing appraisal of deconstruction's place in the humanities. Even before the death of its founder Jacques Derrida in 2004, deconstruction – broadly, the practice of overturning implicit "oppositions" in texts, or indeed in entire systems of thought – had been absorbed by a diverse array of academic disciplines. During the last decades of his life, Derrida's ideas spread not only to literary and cultural studies, but as far afield as legal theory and even theology. There was even talk of a "religious turn" in deconstruction, and in Derrida's work in particular.

Radical Atheism, a bold and iconoclastic book, argued that "all attempts to assimilate Derrida's thinking to a religious framework" were hopelessly "wrongheaded." Christian thinkers like John D. Caputo had drawn comparisons between Derrida's discourse and the similarly slippery language of apophatic or "negative" theology, in which words can only circle around a God whose name remains ineffable. Hägglund, however, held that such religious readings ignored Derrida's deep commitment to atheism. Far from gesturing at an ungraspable transcendence (the "unknown God" of apophaticism) Hägglund demonstrated that deconstruction was firmly focused on the finitude of human life. Not only that, but religion, in reaching toward such transcendence – in its "desire for immortality" – was itself simply a "dissimulation" of a deeper "desire for survival." That is, religion may strive to surpass the transience of temporal life, but, in so doing, it discloses an inescapable investment in it. In the last analysis, religion is rooted in our primal drive to go on living.

Derrida's fans and critics alike are fond of quoting his famous claim, put forward in his 1967 book *Of Grammatology*, that "there is nothing outside of the text" (*"il n'y a pas de hors-texte"*) and for many his name remains related to a somewhat outmoded "linguistic turn" in philosophy, recently much scorned by metaphysically inclined thinkers like Alain Badiou and Quentin Meillassoux. By contrast, *Radical Atheism* redescribed Derrida as a thinker for whom "there can be nothing beyond mortality," and who was less involved with "language for language's sake" than with life as it is lived. The political theorist Ernesto Laclau remarked that Hägglund's argument had approached "the zero degree of deconstruction," a bottom line that could not be "assimilated" to theology or any other supervening discourse. Indeed, in Hägglund's hands deconstruction isn't reductively "discursive" at all. Instead, it's aligned with the most essential level of human experience: that of living and dying, and of the desires to which they give rise.

Hence, Hägglund could be said to have brought deconstruction "back to life." His latest book, *Dying for Time*, further develops his revitalized version of Derrida's thought. This time around though, Hägglund hones in on an area rather less abstract than theology. *Dying for Time* is largely a work of literary criticism, concerned with what another deconstructive critic, Jonathan Culler, once called "the concrete and exemplary dramas of literature." Unlike theology or philosophy, literature can be considered "concrete and exemplary" insofar as it enacts and illuminates lived experience, tracking the texture of our everyday desires and dilemmas. And crucially, for Hägglund, deconstructive criticism, too, must keep close to this texture. As he states at the outset of *Dying for Time*, deconstruction "is not simply an extrinsic theory" that can be "applied" to literary texts. Instead it must be "derived" from those texts, just as they are themselves derived from our experience of "fundamental questions of life and death, time and space, memory and forgetting."

Dying for Time revolves around close readings of canonical novels by Marcel Proust, Virginia Woolf, and Vladimir Nabokov. Broadly speaking, these three novelists could be called "modernist," in at least one sense: each sought to reconfigure literature's representation of time. Modernism, as Baudelaire memorably remarked, tends to express an essential tension between "the transient, the fleeting" on one side, and "the eternal; the immutable" on the other. On the one hand, modernist writers strive to isolate specific instants or sensations: what Woolf called "moments of being," and Joyce "epiphanies." On the other, such moments may seem to evoke an otherworldly eternity. For example, Joyce identifies his epiphanies with earthly reality; they are "the most evanescent of moments," fragile and fleeting, like life itself. Yet he also hints that these epiphanies amount to "a spiritual manifestation" of immortal bliss, as is implicit in the idea's religious root. Hägglund's contention is that literary critics have been misled by this latter theological impulse into finding a false transcendence within modernism. As he argues, "epiphany still tends to be aligned with a supposed experience of timelessness," so that modernism "continues to be read in accordance with a desire for immortality."

To make modernism committedly mortal, despite its apparent desire to be otherwise: this is Hägglund's aim in *Dying for Time.* His argument hinges on a newly-minted concept he calls (recalling Derrida's own fondness for striking coinages) "chrono-libido." Put simply, the theory of chronolibido recapitulates *Radical Atheism*'s claim that *all* desire, especially the religious desire for immortality, is bound up with a basic "investment in survival." Even when we seek to transcend time, we do so because our time-bound lives can be lost. Our finitude is the foundation for all our desires, and all our fears. In fact, desire and fear – *philia* and *phobia* – form the flipsides of chronolibido, as Hägglund explains:

> My key argument concerns the co-implication of *chronophobia* and *chronophilia*. The fear of time and death… is generated by the investment in a life that can be lost. It is because one is attached to a temporal being (chronophilia) that one fears losing it (chronophobia)… It is *because* the beloved can be lost that one seeks to keep it, and it is *because* the experience can be forgotten that one seeks to remember it.

So when we wish, like Plato did, to step out of time into a state of eternal repose, we don't really realize *why* we wish this. There is a way in which we cannot wish for, or care for, anything without a prior awareness that nothing will last.

Hägglund's approach to Proust provides perhaps the best example of "chronolibidinal" criticism in action. First he surveys almost all of the landmark studies of *À la recherche du temps perdu*, and finds them wanting. (One of the joys of Hägglund's work is his willingness to venture this sort of sweeping, bravura critique.) From Georges Poulet to Gilles Deleuze, Proust scholarship has, says Hägglund, mistaken the famed "involuntary memories" of Marcel, the book's protagonist, for revelations of a "timeless essence." What's more, when Marcel himself speaks of memory as "extra-temporal," Hägglund counters that such claims "are contradicted by the logic of the text." This is a classic deconstructive move: reading a text against itself, so as to deflate the received ideas of other readers. For Hägglund, then, even when Marcel's memories appear to free him from time and death, their effect is in fact to "recall him to the pathos of mortal life." This pathos reaches its peak when memory shades into mourning, as in a passage where Marcel remembers his dead grandmother:

Lost forever; I could not understand, and I struggled to endure the pain of this contradiction: on the one hand, an existence, a tenderness, surviving in me such as I had known them... On the other hand, as soon as I had relived, as though present, that felicity, to feel it traversed by the certainty, springing up like a repeated physical pain, of a nothingness that had effaced my image of that tenderness, had destroyed that existence.

In Proust's novel, Hägglund writes, memories of life are always also memories of loss. Even the most ecstatic recollection returns us to a world in which the remembered object is no more. Moreover, this is as true of our memories of ourselves as it is of our memories of others. Our lifetimes, too, are traversed by "nothingness," since every moment we live through "must extinguish itself as soon as it comes." Time is always passing away, each successive second negating the one before, such that "the present itself can come into being only by ceasing to be." In this sense, "extinction is at work in survival itself." Thus the epiphanies we find in Proust do not transcend time. Rather, these memories retrieve the ambivalent rhythms of persistence and disappearance that animate actual life. Proust's real revelation is not that memory makes us immortal, but that life is at all times destructible.

In a subsequent chapter, Woolf's "moments of being" meet a similar treatment. Time and again, Woolf's writing tries (in the words of her classic novel *To the Lighthouse*) "to crystallize and transfix the moment." In that book, the painter Lily Briscoe seeks "to feel simply: that's a chair, that's a table, and yet at the same time, it's a miracle, it's an ecstasy." But to fill fleeting sights and sounds with significance is not to imbue them with "timeless presence," as some readers of Woolf have assumed. Woolf's privileged moments, like Proust's memories, can't help but reveal "how even the most immediate presence passes away." Not only this: in Woolf temporality becomes *traumatic*, brutally attuned to the terror of transience. Clarissa Dalloway lives her life as a chain of charged moments which leave her full of "divine vitality" and at the same time "alone against the appalling night... suddenly shriveled and aged." For Hägglund the two go hand in hand, since "the pathos of Woolf's *moments of living* stems from the fact that they are always already *moments of dying*." So, Woolf shows us how living in time is at once chronophilic and chronophobic: her characters' encounters with existence are

> not moments of timeless plenitude, but testify to the inherent traumatism of temporal life. They may intensify one's attachment to life... but they may equally well shatter one's attachment to life and make survival unbearable.

Hägglund's analysis of Nabokov highlights writing itself, an act which could be considered continuous with our lived experience of time. Since it attempts to preserve its content for posterity, writing is clearly a chronolibidinal practice *par excellence*. But while Nabokov's scholarly commentators have supposed that "his writing is driven by a desire to transcend time," Hägglund has a more nuanced model in mind. For him, all writing is radically corruptible: to put pen to paper is to risk slips, mistakes, misinterpretations.

Nabokov's late novel *Ada or Ardor* is a case in point. The book recounts the reunion of Van and Ada, two siblings whose incestuous love story is told by means of Van's memoirs. But what Van has written is incomplete, as well as being incessantly interrupted by notes and revisions – his own, Ada's, and those of an unnamed editor. "Far from redeeming corruptibility," therefore, writing here "highlights that inscription is inseparable from the risk of erasure." Under such conditions, even Van's most treasured memories – like that of when he and Ada first made love – dissipate into doubt and vagueness: "Summer 1960?

Crowded hotel somewhere between Ex and Ardez?" When writing records and recalls times like these, the very "process of preservation" prolongs their exposure to "the threat of oblivion." In this way, rather than transcending time, to write only ever deepens our investment in a double-edged struggle of "survival" and "disappearance."

Dying for Time delivers a revolutionary reading of the ways in which modernist writers express elemental aspects of human existence. In the process, it disproves the idea that deconstruction – or, indeed, literary theory *per se* – is always offputtingly arid and abstract. Hägglund's approach is absolutely the opposite, attuned at all times to "the impossibility of being indifferent to survival." Whether or not there is nothing outside of the text, Hägglund puts texts back in touch with the "terror and beauty" of being briefly alive; of being able to "suffer, lose things, and die," and thereby knowing "what it means for something to be precious." This is a book that brings literature and theory into forceful collision with life's underlying realities. The resulting insight is resolutely atheistic: neither art nor thought allow access to another world of timeless perfection. Instead, each is irreducibly interwoven with the world in which we live. Some say that literary theory is dead, out of fashion, a thing of the past. But Hägglund shows how it can and should go on living: in unflinching fidelity to how it feels to be human.

A Way of Life that Withdraws from Life

Peter Sloterdijk, *The Art of Philosophy:*
Wisdom as a Practice

Philosophy, as Pierre Hadot once put it, is perhaps less a body of knowledge than a "way of life." If this is so, it follows that philosophers shouldn't be overly idealistic about their ideas. Such ideas are embedded not only in broad social contexts, but in philosophers' own self-understandings; in their acts of self-fashioning. And to the extent that this existential dimension remains largely repressed or unthematized, the discipline stands in a state of reflexive deficit. In this respect, what we require is a materialist theory of philosophy: a robust redescription of contemplation as, first and foremost, an embodied practice.

For Peter Sloterdijk, such practices properly belong to the sphere of "anthropotechnics." In his bestselling book *You Must Change Your Life*, Sloterdijk defines this terrain as "the tableau of human 'work on oneself'... a region that can be referred to with such categories as education, etiquette, custom, habit formation, training and exercise." *The Art of Philosophy* brings precisely this perspective to bear on the stances and attitudes that underwrite science, scholarship, and what we unthinkingly call "the life of the mind." Seen in this light, such a life looks newly unusual:

> If the theoretical attitude is to be a matter of practice, then the cardinal exercise would be a withdrawal exercise. It would be an exercise in not-taking-up-a-position, an attempt at the art of suspending participation in life in the midst of life.

The life of the mind is a way of life that withdraws from life. This is the central thesis of Sloterdijk's striking book, whose title in

157

German is the more apposite *Scheintod im Denken* – 'Suspended Animation in Thought." Sloterdijk starts with Plato's account of Socrates, for whom philosophical thought took the form of "a trance or obsessive daydream." In short, Socrates was sometimes literally "lost in thought," gripped by a kind of "artificial autism" – an ascetic secession from social life into the realm of ideas. To think, for Socrates, was to be dead to the world. Accordingly, Sloterdijk relocates the root of "the ancient European culture of rationality" in "the idea that the thinking person is a kind of dead person on holiday."

This statement's irreverence is instructive. By his own admission, Sloterdijk is intentionally "hyperbolic," and hardly a slave to scholarly standards. Like several of his shorter texts, *The Art of Philosophy* started life as a lecture: a form in which intellectual substance isn't straightforwardly separable from rhetorical strategy. It's unclear whether Sloterdijk's writing could itself be called "philosophy," but perhaps this accounts for its polemical power. His style circumvents any single disciplinary discourse. Instead, it comes from a place where such canons can be creatively combined, ironized, or iconoclastically attacked.

In consequence, Sloterdijk quite often brings a bracing anti-academicism to his arguments. *The Art of Philosophy* is no exception. Taking up an old idea of Nietzsche's, the book portrays the founding of Plato's Academy as a retreat from a failing Athenian political culture: "a reaction to the collapse of the *polis*." On this reading, philosophical or theoretical life – the *bios theoretikós* – arose in response to the death throes of democracy. Since then, academe has always been about "shutting out the world," for better or worse. And as for the "love of wisdom," says Sloterdijk, "it was the first and purest form of loser romanticism, reinterpreting a defeat as a victory on another field."

Later, this rubric of "loser romanticism," itself reminiscent of Nietzsche's notion of *ressentiment*, inspires an incisive foray into the psychology of theory. For Sloterdijk, the people most prone to take flight into theory are those "who seem lost in the world." But by looking closely at this loss, this "low-level alienation," we can cast theory's unworldly ideals under suspicion. So, Sloterdijk calls for a critical genealogy of the "theorist" as a character type:

> What if the much-lauded theoretical virtues really derive from secret weaknesses? What if they're based on a questionable compensation for stubborn defects, or even on the morbid inability to face the facts of life without embell-ishment and evasion? Does homo theoreticus really come from such a good background as he has assured us from his earliest days? Or is he actually a bastard trying to impress us with fake titles?

Surely some of us will see ourselves – and laugh at ourselves – in what Sloterdijk calls his "portrait of the theoretician as a young man." Nonetheless, theoretical life needn't always be damaged life. As Sloterdijk explains, "a definitive exposure of theory as 'nothing but' compensation for something better... cannot succeed." Clearly then, his approach isn't crudely reductive. Far from being a one-sided critique, the book becomes ever more flexibly essayistic, mapping the philosophical mindset in all its ambiguous "happiness and misery."

The Art of Philosophy ends in the present era, in which "episte-mological modernism" has demystified many of the "exalted fictions of disinterested reason." From Marx to Sartre to Bourdieu, modernity has at least partly recoupled cognition to concrete customs, promising a "liquidation of the ancient European subject of theory." But for all this, traces of "suspended animation" still survive, as do "distant glimpses" of Socrates' sacred absences of mind. And so they should, resolves Sloterdijk. Philosophy can't be conclusively purged of its ascetic inheri-tance. But perhaps we can conceive of a world in which philosophy's past is repurposed; put in pursuit of a way of life

that is "neither merely active nor merely contemplative" –
wisdom as a new kind of practice.

Voices for the Voiceless

Jacques Rancière, *Mute Speech and Staging
the People* vols. 1 and 2

With its leading lights now all but gone out, the fashion-conscious field of "French theory" stands in need of some new stars. At the moment, one of the main attractions is Jacques Rancière, subject of a swelling list of translations, and a darling not just of the Anglophone academy, but also, interestingly, of the art world. While known for his link (and subsequent split) with Louis Althusser, in some ways Rancière may be more reminiscent of Michel Foucault. Like the latter, he's often frustratingly opaque, but with flashes of counterintuitive brilliance, and a knack for turning commonplace concepts on their heads. His recent work has redescribed aesthetics in terms of a "distribution of the sensible," probing into the politics of the way that art arranges perception.

The recently translated *Mute Speech* marks Rancière's most sustained application of his aesthetic theory to literature, and to literary history. In broad terms, the book locates the birth of our current conception of literature in the transition from neoclassical to modern aesthetics. But to put the point this simply does it a disservice. Rancière isn't retreading some tired routine about a naive realism overthrown by a revolutionary modernism. Rather, he argues, writing's "representative" and "expressive" roles relate not to periods but to aesthetic "regimes" that overlap, and that aren't always at odds with each other.

In the regime of French neoclassical poetry, writing is restricted by rules of decorum. Enacting a sort of analogy between texts and the social structure surrounding them, decorum distributes styles of writing inside a strict hierarchy of genres, anxiously measuring their appropriateness. As Rancière says, in neoclassicism "what is wrong is always unsuitable." Yet this sets the stage for a paradigm shift; for the eruption of something unsuited to "the normative system of *belles lettres*." As it turns out, Rancière's favored example of this is Victor Hugo's *Notre-Dame de Paris*. What makes that book radical, Rancière claims, is its depersonalization of speech. That is, instead of decorously dealing out speech among speakers, Hugo's narrative allows Notre Dame to speak for itself, mutely, in its own unspoken "language of stone." Uncoupled from any human source, this voiceless voice disrupts the order of things, setting a dangerous precedent. From now on, a notion of unanchored "absolute" writing will threaten the representative function of literature.

Rancière is refreshingly unorthodox in unearthing examples of "mute speech" not from modernism, but from relatively prosaic realist and naturalist novels. It isn't the avant-garde, but boring old realism that triggers the breakdown of genres into an "anarchy of writing." Indeed, realist novels pioneer a new impropriety, since they imply, for the first time, a writer who writes "for those who should not read him." One wishes here for a few reflections on the nineteenth-century reading public; on the social correlatives of the rise of the novel. Unfortunately, when Rancière calls literature "democratic," he's guided not by a history of reading, but by his own rather less relevant reading of Plato's *Phaedrus*. On the back of a Socratic grumble about writing's social disorderliness, he suggests that the written word is *essentially* revolutionary, given its errant tendency to float free of its origins, to circulate, and to lend itself to appropriation. But surely this slip into linguistic idealism reveals a slight weakness in his argument. A theory of "mute" speech can hardly afford much importance to real speakers and listeners, and one wonders how worthwhile it is to attribute more agency to writing than to those whose lives are linked with it. Isn't literary history driven less by abstractions than by real reading and writing practices, demographic factors, and the pace of technological change?

For those who like a little more history with their theory, Verso's two volumes of Rancière's earlier writings may be more gratifying. The essays that make up *Staging the People* and its companion piece *The Intellectual and his People* are drawn from the legendary journal *Les Révoltes logiques* (1975–81), a short-lived forum for some fascinating work in French labor history. Halfway between academia and activism, *Les Révoltes* was set up to take stock of the political failure of May 1968. Returning to the nineteenth century, it sought to explore the explanatory gap between socialist theory and the reality of workers' social movements. Rancière's contributions to *Les Révoltes* reflect his concern to reconstruct the lived complexity of working class culture, against the "austere proletariat of Marxist theory," but also against romantic nostalgia.

The Intellectual and his People contains some remarkably sharp interventions against thinkers who misleadingly claim to "speak for" the masses. One notable essay attacks the so-called *nouveaux philosophes*, who led French culture's break with the left in the wake of 1968. André Glucksmann's manifesto for this movement, *La Cuisinière et le mangeur d'hommes*, is singled out for a skilfully savage review. Rancière ridicules Glucksmann's reductive assertion that "Marx was responsible for the gulag," and goes on to show how such anti-Marxist rhetoric is no less dogmatic than the doctrine it purports to oppose. In Rancière's view, Glucksmann and his allies merely exchange Marxism's flawed model of the proletariat for their own equally naive notion of "the people." Indeed the *nouveaux philosophes*, like Pierre Bourdieu (who also comes in for criticism in this collection) belong to an intellectual lineage which, since Plato, has only spoken for the people by keeping them silent. In this tradition, the people's real purpose is to underwrite the authority of their spokesmen. For Rancière, all of this serves to suppress historical truth. Glucksmann's posturing is therefore "less important in what it says than in what it stops us from looking at... against its story, we should try to relearn our own history."

The archival research recounted in *Staging the People* is rich in historical detail, ranging from the Californian gold rush to the Paris Exposition of 1867. The standout article is invitingly titled "Good Times, Or, Pleasure at the *Barrière*." Here Rancière roams through the social spaces of nineteenth-century Paris, from the drinking dens of the city limits to informal "café theatres" where the bourgeoisie briefly mingled with off-duty workers. Complicating our orthodox picture of classes pitted against one another, the essay maps a "half-fantastic geography of inter-class exchanges" that blurs the boundaries between labor and leisure, high and low culture. An especially evocative section traces the way that song lyrics were transformed in their travels through the city, taking new shapes in the improvisations and interventions of the café-concert scene. In such situations, a worker could be "radicalized" by getting artistic ideas above his station. Thus, against a crudely oppositional counterculture, Rancière superbly reclaims the subtle disruptiveness of the parvenu, and the autodidact. Of course, such social slippages were just as subtly policed, and the café-concerts themselves were finally privatized via the gramophone, a device whose prerecorded pleasures put an end to "a thousand games of social theatricality."

In retrospect, Rancière's early scholarship adds some much-needed empirical meat to the bones of his mature, more theoretical work. Indeed, it might even help to historicize his abstract musings in *Mute Speech* on the rebelliousness of the "wandering letter." *Staging the People* is particularly welcome in this respect, since its play of proletarian voices clearly and concretely illustrates how words can forge new distributions of the sensible. Perhaps it is telling, then, that this line of argument makes so much more sense when it's embedded in thick descriptions of social reality. One of the lessons of Rancière's work, and one of the problems with which it reflexively contends, is that an account of the political power of language may be best supported by other sources than those drawn from the canons of literature, or, for that matter, of philosophy.

Philosophical Myths and Memories

Peter E. Gordon, *Continental Divide:*
Heidegger, Cassirer, Davos

Philosophy, it could be said, constructs itself in retrospect; thought acquires meaning by means of its memories. Indeed, writes Peter Gordon, perhaps what all philosophies have in common is that each "comes to understand itself by telling itself stories about where it has been." From the trial of Socrates to Wittgenstein's poker-wielding quarrel with Popper, such stories form the fabric of "philosophical memory," a kind of cultural-cognitive process whereby concepts are coded with historical content. In the so-called "continental" tradition, few remembered moments have come to seem more meaningful than the 1929 "Davos dispute" between Martin Heidegger and Ernst Cassirer. At that time, the two men ranked among Europe's most eminent intellectuals. The theme of the meeting that brought them together was the ambitious question, "What is the Human Being?" Accordingly, their encounter was seen as broadly symbolic of everything from the then nascent crisis within neo-Kantianism to a conflict between, in Karl Mannheim's sense, culturally irreconcilable "generations." In the eighty years between then and now, the Davos exchange has played its part in some of the grandest narratives of modern intellectual history – not least Michael Friedman's influential account of a "parting of the ways"; a supposed separation of analytic from continental philosophical styles.

For all this, though, what if such retroactive readings have misrepresented the event's real import? After all, in philosophical as in other forms of memory, the associative (not to mention emotive) act of remembering all too often colors a memory's content. In this way, by extension, it's easy to see how entire disciplines could end up overdetermined by their own self-descriptions. What's more, a measure of interpretive violence is done when a debate like Davos is made to serve as a sign of broader political significance. A case in point would be Bourdieu's take on it, in his *The Political Ontology of Martin Heidegger*. Here the conceptual core of the encounter is crudely hollowed out in order to portray philosophy as an allegory of social power. Surely, to analyze Heidegger's (or Cassirer's) arguments by way of such a sociology is already to instrumentalize them. Instead, reasons Gordon, the best bet for both philosophy *and* politics would be to divest the fetishized memory of Davos of any such "allegorical function." With Davos, what was once a dialogue has long since ossified into a fixational fable. Hence, what history requires is a reflexive, disenchanted reading, in which all second-order stories (be they sweepingly socio-political or insularly professional) are briefly bracketed out, at least to begin with. Space is then cleared for a more careful contextualization, where meaning may be gradually reconstructed from the ground up.

For Gordon, what grounded the Davos debate was a conceptual conflict between "two normative images of humanity." (A "normative image" is the unthematized picture that precedes any intellectual position; "an intuitive notion that provides an initial sense of orientation.") Hence, Heidegger's arguments were animated by an image of humanity's "thrownness" (*Geworfenheit*) – for him, Dasein was inescapably finite, situated inside its existential horizon. Cassirer, by contrast, clung to a neo-Kantian notion of mental "spontaneity" – of man's expressive ability to structure his field of experience, pressing beyond the condition of "being there" towards a truly objective symbolic order. All this could look like a simplification, of course, insofar as it boils down to a binary gloss (Enlightenment humanism versus existentialist fatalism; metaphysical *angst* against anthropological agency) but it serves

Gordon well as a way of concretizing the exchange's conceptual framework. With the stage thus set, what happened next (and what Davos perhaps demonstrates *par excellence*) was a process that Gordon calls "ramification." If we recall that to "operationalize" a concept is to set limits to its extension, to watch it "ramify" is, Gordon says, to see it "branch out into the wider world," amassing a freight of associations which "magnify its rhetorical force and cultural-historical significance." This is the slow slippage from normative image to narrative; the diffusion by which Davos became a mythical *point of reference*.

Gordon's "ramified" concepts appear roughly similar to what the sociologist Niilo Kauppi has called "power-ideas." One common thrust of both of these theories is that the more associative links an idea can consolidate for itself, the more leverage it will have in the intellectual field as a whole, mobilizing its clusters of connotations so as to achieve a "metapreferential" priority over competing concepts. In the Heidegger-Cassirer conflict, this comparison is borne out by the ways in which both philosophers tried to *negatively* ramify each other's habits of mind. Cassirer implicitly classed Heidegger as an outdated metaphysician, while Heidegger "inscribed" Cassirer into his own "larger and more ramified cultural-metaphysical narrative," that of the *Seinsvergessenheit*, philosophy's forgetting of Being. So, each subjected the other's stance to adverse ramification through "historical redescription." Gordon appears to claim that such moves are not philosophically valid, but this begs the question of why historicity should not (indeed, how it cannot) be at stake in argumentation. In any case, though, a degree of "philosophical one-upmanship," as he puts it, clearly seems to have taken place. Throughout the debate, both speakers' statements were rhetorically underscored by "arguments for priority," consisting not only of conflicting narrativizations (that is, each placed himself at a more advanced stage in philosophical *history*) but also of vying metaphilosophies. In that of Cassirer, "the transcendental method must serve as *the general point of departure for all philosophical problems*," whereas for Heidegger, of course, that privileged part was played by "fundamental" ontology. In this sense, then, each opponent positioned his own ideas as conditions of intelligibility for those of his interlocutor.

Gordon's close attention to the rhetorical implicature of the Davos debate is deeply illuminating. Unlike other analyses, it pinpoints the problem of the participants' failure to find a "common language" in which to formalize their disagreement. That is, in symbolic struggles like the one described above, every layer of figuration further obstructs the constructive conduct of dialogue. If, as Gerald Graff has argued, "making intellectual culture coherent... requires foregrounding points of controversy," then one could say of Davos that the rapid ramification of the conversation's content was precisely what prevented a fully adequate foregrounding. Instead, and especially in the decades that followed, the disagreement was displaced onto the indeterminate domain of "ideological effects" and "cultural consequences" (as in later indictments of the elective affinities between Heidegger's *Existenzphilosophie* and his Nazism). What was lost in translation during this interpretive shift "from conceptual truth to pragmatic efficacy" was any way of distilling a soluble philosophical conflict from the attendant set of insoluble symbolic ones – the unwieldy idea of an epochal clash between Cassirer's cosmopolitanism and Heidegger's irrational nationalism, for example.

Clearly, the methodology displayed in *Continental Divide* creates some complex entailments. At one point, Gordon explains that the book has been guided by a drive to "sustain the distinction between philosophy and history." He then goes on to reflect that

one might say it is a desideratum for philosophy that its arguments should be resolved by philosophical means only and without reference to the non-philosophical world. On this view, philosophy would seem to demand a kind of *askesis*, the principled attempt to hold thought apart from all that is mundane.

As a formula for doing philosophy, the value of this ascetic ideal seems far from self-evident; a more honest desideratum might ask for quite the opposite. Anyway, as Gordon goes on to point out, the principle may well be unrealizable, as every philosophical concept "begins to ramify the instant it is conceived." So, the kind of distillation described above can't quite be accomplished, since "there is no moment of pure thought that does not immediately take on a further meaning." But perhaps we could posit that the pursuit of such a pristine moment does remain a latent aim of Gordon's, at least *at the level of method*, existing in a slightly unstable tension with his detailed reading of Davos's long arc of ramification. Whether or not that criticism carries weight, what *Continental Divide* successfully demonstrates is that the essence of Davos was irreducibly philosophical. And even if that essence isn't historically isolable, Gordon firmly establishes that it can't be explained away as an epiphenomenon of some deeper, prior political cause. Nor can any dispute's outcome be decided on the evidence of subsequent allegorizations. In its level-headed argument against these misleading myths and memories, *Continental Divide* clears the ground for new and more thoughtful ways of rendering philosophy's richly entangled relationship with its history.

Strategies of Sense-Making

Martin Woessner, *Heidegger in America*

All too often, philosophers act as if their arguments were autonomous from non-philosophical factors. In this sense, philosophy's default position is remarkably unreflexive. Yet recent years have seen several scholars turn their attention to the reception of philosophy, rather than its internal logic. Studies such as George Cotkin's *Existential America*, François Cusset's *French Theory*, and Jennifer Ratner-Rosenhagen's *American Nietzsche* have helped reconnect philosophy to the historical situations which condition its interpretation. The best of these books carefully follow the course of philosophical ideas as they cross between contexts, and indeed continents. In each case, the hope is to historicize such ideas, instead of explicitly evaluating them. As Peter Gordon has put it, if philosophy deals in proof and refutation, this kind of intellectual history has at its heart a more modest method of "understanding."

Martin Woessner's *Heidegger in America* marks a major contribution to this field. The book, Woessner writes, maps "how Heidegger was (re)made in the U.S.A," reconstructing his "American reception" from the 1930s to the present. It is a work of what Woessner calls "reception history" – a case study in the transnational exchange of ideas. The latter is a complex and contradictory process, often beset by, as Pierre Bourdieu has put it, "structural misunderstandings." Unsurprisingly then, studies of this sort are difficult to define and delimit. Woessner has his work cut out for him, as Heidegger's American reception ranges widely within and beyond the academy, from philosophy and theology to architecture and popular culture. *Heidegger in America* covers all this ground and more. In doing so, though, could it be criticized for being too diffuse? Woessner would argue not. He sees this inclusivity as vital to understanding his subject. As he asserts, "reception studies take as their central task the narration of diffusion."

Indeed, the value of this ambitious book lies in its adaptable description of diffusion. Chapter by chapter, Woessner charts a rich empirical exposition of Heidegger's influence. Yet the insights this yields can be extrapolated, contributing to a more general model of philosophical dissemination. The opening chapters are a case in point. Here Woessner researches Heidegger's earliest American interlocutors, including Charles Hartshorne and Marjorie Grene. He unearths from their work a common hostility to Heidegger's "cheap rhetoric," to adopt Grene's words. This thread is picked up again in a 1948 essay by Günther Stern, "On the Pseudo-Concreteness of Heidegger's Philosophy." The article attacks Heidegger's *Dasein* as a hollow abstraction, "far from any actual living, breathing human entity." Thus, in condemning Heidegger's project as "an existential account with the existence left out," Stern links the line of critique begun by Grene and Hartshorne to later polemics like Adorno's *The Jargon of Authenticity*. For Woessner, this genealogy demonstrates a generalizable principle: "reception is not synonymous with adulation." If philosophy spreads via the vector of commentary, it does so no matter how negatively it is valorized. This might begin to explain how attacks against a given philosophy can nonetheless play a functional role in securing its circulation.

A chapter on "Exiles and Emissaries" considers the part played by German émigré intellectuals in disseminating Heidegger's thought throughout the US. Richard Wolin has already plotted this topic in his book *Heidegger's Children*, focusing on famous names like Arendt and Marcuse. But Woessner fills in Wolin's omissions, discussing lesser-known "stepchildren" like the historian Paul Kristeller. What emerges from this approach is an analysis of the "personal" or pre-philosophical dimension of reception. Heidegger's protégés engaged with his work in the context of their prior engagements with his "charismatic persona," encountered primarily through his pedagogy. His diffusion was therefore secured not so much by his thought as by his intellectual aura; his "style of thinking." Hence it makes sense to speak of former students like Leo Strauss as "methodological Heideggerians," whose work reflects their teacher's dispositions more than his doctrine. As Woessner writes,

> What Heidegger's students absorbed, after all, was not a specific dogma, but a methodology that was rooted in a specific philosophical attitude or style. What unites thinkers as different as Kristeller and Strauss is a mode of thinking... a conception of the philosophical persona itself.

Woessner's book has many merits, but this may be its most valuable claim. The emphasis on "modes of thinking" suggests a reshaping of reception history, not merely as a "study of textual migrations," but as an inquiry into the social psychology of intellectuals. What schemas, what strategies of sense-making, would lead one to identify oneself, consciously or not, as a Heideggerian? Such identifications are produced partly by the "performative" aspects of academic culture – as Woessner notes, Heidegger's diffusion must have had something to do with his "mesmerizing presence behind the lectern." The hidden curriculum transmitted in such cases of "charismatic pedagogy" is not a formalized philosophy but what Woessner calls a "philosophical persona" – a specific conception, led by example, of what it means to *be* a philosopher.

The sociologist Neil Gross has sketched what such personae look like, with his theory of "intellectual self-concepts." But perhaps Gross puts too much stress on self-fashioning, as if intellectuals' identities arose solely from their own biographies. In contrast, Woessner shows how self-concepts are themselves iterable, reproduced between master-thinkers and their disciples. If styles of writing spread through citation and imitation, underlying intellectual stances don't evolve in isolation either. Identities are equally transmissible; indeed, at one level, identity and style are indissoluble. Woessner later shows how this sheds light on the legendary "Davos debate" between Heidegger and Cassirer. Davos can be recast, he claims, as a performative clash whose stakes were as much attitudinal as philosophical. The encounter's lasting influence lay in its counterposing of two self-concepts, which then re-emerged as mutually exclusive images for American philosophers to identify with: "the philosopher as scientist versus the philosopher as seer." For Woessner, these personae fed into today's perceived fissure between "analytic" and "continental" philosophy.

Although Woessner is at his strongest when he explores these psychological schemas, his study never neglects the structural importance of institutions. Notably, he highlights how Heidegger's academic institutionalization first occurred in theology departments, through the work of religious thinkers like Paul Tillich and William Richardson. Only later would it undergo a "process of secularization," enabling it to be embedded in the philosophical profession. To be sure, the first English translation of *Being and Time*, by John Macquarrie and Edward Robinson, was initially published by a religious imprint. In this respect it seems correct for Woessner to claim that "Heidegger's relevance to theology was his entry ticket into American intellectual debate."

Even so, this institutional angle only tells one side of the story. With Heidegger, such a description has to be thickened by an account of popular culture. Here Woessner rightly reminds us that the "high seriousness" of philosophers and theologians has been paralleled by diffusions in "different registers," ranging from literary references to the films of Heidegger translator Terrence Malick. Of special significance, though, is the popular portrayal of Heidegger as an "existentialist." As Randall Collins has argued in his *The Sociology of Philosophies*, existentialism is less a philosophy than a "philosophical-literary hybrid," whose channels of diffusion differ from those of more narrowly "academic" ideas. Existentialism is a mass-market phenomenon, with access to a wider variety of reproductive apparatuses. Of these, Woessner draws attention to a wave of "paperback existentialism," embodied in affordable anthologies like Walter Kaufmann's *Existentialism from Dostoyevsky to Sartre*. As Woessner reveals, Heidegger's inclusion in this pop-cultural canon was a crucial condition of his reception.

Heidegger in America surveys a vast terrain, and at times it strains to marshal its materials. Reception studies tend to tread a fine line between mere description and an overly dogmatic deduction of patterns. For the most part however, Woessner masterfully combines historical detail with a conceptual grasp of what his different contexts have in common. For instance, separate sections on Hubert Dreyfus, Richard Rorty, and Allan Bloom (author of the anti-Heideggerian *The Closing of the American Mind*) depict several disparate uses to which Heidegger's thought has been put. But while Woessner sums up the specifics of these examples, he's also able to step back and assess their resemblances. Hence, he hints that where each of these thinkers read Heidegger for his own ends, each shared the same meta-intellectual strategy; the same way of rendering Heidegger's thought as an appropriable epistemic resource. By historicizing the field in which such appropriations occurred, Woessner gives us a valuable guide to the dynamics of Heidegger's diffusion. Yet the strength of his study is that its insights also apply to other philosophers, in other places and times. From now on, we might say of many such thinkers what Woessner says of Heidegger: that he "authored the script, but others ultimately gave the performances."

Belief from Non-Belief

Simon Critchley, *The Faith of the Faithless:*
Experiments in Political Theology

Simon Critchley, a British philosopher based at The New School in New York, is best known for books like *Very Little... Almost Nothing*, *Infinitely Demanding*, and *The Book of Dead Philosophers*, a bestseller that has helped to cement his status as a prominent public intellectual. (Recently this status was further solidified by a noteworthy spat between Critchley and the Slovenian philosophical superstar Slavoj Žižek, about which more below.) Over the years he's developed a reputation as a rigorous philosopher in the continental tradition, playing a major role in the Anglophone reception of tricky French thinkers like Emmanuel Levinas and Jacques Derrida. Yet he's also proved to be passionate about making philosophy an accessible part of contemporary culture – for instance, through "The Stone," an opinion series he organizes for *The New York Times*.

Throughout his career, Critchley has recast philosophy as a response to two types of "disappointment": the *religious* (how are we to deal with life after the death of God?) and the *political* (what's left for the Left to rally around, in light of the apparent triumph of neoliberalism?) His latest book, *The Faith of the Faithless*, systematically connects these two threads. We live, Critchley claims, in an age defined by a "dangerous interdependence of politics and religion," where warfare is underwritten by overt religious rhetoric. "Somehow we seem to have passed," he observes,

> from a secular age, which we were ceaselessly told was post-metaphysical, to a new situation in which political action seems to flow directly from metaphysical conflict... in which

religiously justified violence is the means to a political end.

But if today's violent conflicts – in the Middle East, for instance – are connected to a "clash of fundamentalisms," this, for Critchley, is only a symptom of something more deep-rooted. Indeed, our religious and political disappointments could turn out to be inextricable, for Critchley contends that politics *per se* is religious; and *The Faith of the Faithless* makes a compelling case for this claim.

Critchley begins the book by unpicking a typically knotty epigram from Oscar Wilde: "Everything to be true must become a religion." His first philosophical feat is to show us why we should take this *bon mot* seriously. If we're to appreciate religion's political power, we must understand how belief imbues ideas with truth; how faith lends weight to an argument. For Critchley, Wilde's riddle has something to tell us about why beliefs, even the secular sort, are so often wrapped up in a "framework of ritual." Even our most rational beliefs are brought about partly through faith; they're religious in structure. So, secular creeds must mimic religious ones if they're to be taken as true.

Putting Wilde's words to work on world politics, Critchley turns to the tradition known as "political theology," a subject best summed up by Carl Schmitt in his book of the same name. In that work, Schmitt declares that "all significant concepts in the modern theory of the state are secularized theological concepts." For Critchley, these words resonate with Wilde's aphorism, shedding light on how "political forms" – from fascism to liberalism – are fashioned out of the raw materials of faith. Put simply, there's a covert religious core to all kinds of political life. And if there's something of the "church" inside every "state," then states can only hope to survive if they're *sanctified* in some way. Critchley uncovers a classic example of this in *The Social Contract*, where Jean-Jacques Rousseau's blueprint for secular states runs into trouble when it attempts to cement the state's legal legitimacy. In the end, it can only do so by granting the state the same "sacred" status as a deity. In Rousseau's words (which, again, parallel Wilde's) "it would require gods to give men laws."

With these literary and philosophical authorities behind him, Critchley goes on to claim that politics consists of reconfigurations of religion. In this respect, the political realm is partly fictional in nature; it works with what Critchley calls "fictional force." But if politics only becomes possible by founding itself on fictions, then those fictions are nonetheless *necessary*, and needn't always be read negatively (i.e. as lies). Beneath every deceptive dogma, there's always a suppressed potential for other, more "fructuous collisions... between poetry and politics." Crucially, Critchley doesn't think we can disentangle religious fictions from political facts; to attempt to separate one from the other would only mislead us. What we can do, though, is acknowledge and enrich their relationship, recovering the productive power of belief:

> Politics is a kind of magic show, where we know that the rabbit has not miraculously appeared in the empty hat and the magician's charming assistant has not been sawn in half, but where we are willing to suspend disbelief and go along with the illusion – believe!

The optimistic note at the end of this passage is characteristic of Critchley's style of argument. Although an atheist and, in his previous books, a diagnostician of "disappointment," he's by no means a pessimist. Nor is he content to criticize established beliefs without offering, or at least earnestly searching for, constructive alternatives. Perhaps Critchley's philosophy, like that of René Descartes, pursues a path through doubt towards an affirmation of faith. This movement can even be mapped onto the course of his career. His major early work, the neo-nihilist treatise *Very Little... Almost Nothing*, asserted the essential "finitude," or limitedness, of the human condition. But later books, like *Infinitely Demanding*, argued that this finitude could form a foundation for complex ethical commitments. In its way, *The Faith of the Faithless* fulfils the arc of those earlier arguments, fleshing out a positive political philosophy from a "disappointed" premise: nurturing belief from non-belief.

Critchley's optimism is nowhere more moving than in his refutations of authoritarianism, and of the promises of revolutionary violence. The former he reveals to be reliant upon a "redescription of original sin." At the heart of all authoritarian credos, Critchley argues, is a theological fiction: the age-old belief that "human nature is essentially wicked" and that we're thus intrinsically in need of rule and regulation. "The idea of original sin is not some outdated relic from the religious past," he argues,

> which is why authoritarians think that human beings require the yoke of the state, God, law, and the police. Politics becomes the means for protecting human beings from themselves, that is, from their worst inclinations towards lust, cruelty, and violence.

Against this assumption, Critchley insists that we must maintain our faith in human nature; only then can society be reconceived as a "sinless union with others." This insistence makes him, as he puts it, "a utopian and an optimist about what human beings are capable of." Ever since the 1960s, continental philosophers have tended to embrace "the death of man," as both a historical reality and, more problematically, a desideratum. The exciting rhetoric of texts like Roland Barthes' "The Death of the Author" and Michel Foucault's *The Order of Things* (with its final image of man "erased, like a face drawn in sand at the edge of the sea") has ossified into a default, unexamined anti-humanism. Making a clean break with this tradition, *The Faith of the Faithless* sees

Critchley come out as an unabashed humanist.

But humanism in Critchley's hands is all about humility: there's no room for naive heroics in his utopia. These concerns are at the core of his book's most polemical section, in which he adds further fuel to his ongoing feud with Slavoj Žižek. The backstory here has to do with an article Žižek wrote for the *London Review of Books* a few years ago, criticizing Critchley's support for anti-war and anti-capitalist protests and his advocacy of a "politics of resistance to the state." Žižek's piece, entitled "Resistance is Surrender," asserted that

> today's liberal-democratic state and [Critchley's] dream of an "infinitely demanding" politics exist in a relationship of mutual parasitism. The demonstrations against the US attack on Iraq offer an exemplary case of this strange symbiotic relationship between power and resistance. Both sides were satisfied... the protesters saved their beautiful souls... those in power calmly accepted it.

Peaceful protests only stabilize the status quo, claimed Žižek; what was needed wasn't a show of resistance *to* the state but an aggressive seizure *of* it. Yet Critchley's close reading of Žižek in *The Faith of the Faithless* skilfully shows how the latter's line of argument lapses into "armchair romantic glorifications of revolutionary violence." Žižek emerges in Critchley's account as a politically paralyzed fantasist, in love with a "dream" of brutal revolutionary rupture. That such "absolute, cataclysmic" events can't come about without bloodshed isn't a problem for him, but it clearly remains one for Critchley, as it has been for a long line of British philosophers, going at least as far back as Edmund Burke. In theological terms, Žižek's dream is a little like a miracle. And of course, Critchley is keenly aware of what happens when politics is misdirected by miracles.

So, how would a "faith of the faithless" actually play out in practice? If Critchley quite convincingly fends off his critics, and pinpoints certain logical flaws in a whole lineage of political thinkers, what does he propose in place of the arguments he attacks? As his book's subtitle suggests, he doesn't idealistically dream of achieving an outright escape from "political theology." Instead, he hopes, more modestly, to develop new ways of "experimenting" within it. In so doing he finds a faith which is, he says, "not theistic," which doesn't depend on a deity. Rather, it's rooted in humble human experience, in "imperfection and failure" – indeed, in the essential "finitude" which his earlier work addressed so well. What's more, and unlike Žižek's revolutionary bluster, this formulation of faith is founded upon a strong ethical imperative. It is, Critchley concludes, guided by "the infinite demand of love," and its only dogma is not to do violence to, or to dominate, others. The simplest way of saying this is that Critchley's faith has a strong sense of *conscience*, which he calls "the most enigmatic aspect of what it means to be human." Conscientiously committed, active but pacifistic: *The Faith of the Faithless* provides a powerful vision of what a progressive politics might look like.

No More Great Ideas

Mark M. Freed, *Robert Musil and the NonModern*

In European and American culture of the past two centuries, a sense of rupture pervaded the collective consciousness. The reasons are familiar: revolutions in France and in America; the age of industry; urbanization; class conflict; religious doubt; the spread of empire... taken together, these different dimensions of change converged and accumulated, until a *discourse of novelty* became inescapable.

So writes the literary critic Michael Levenson, in a recent account of the tangled relations between "modernity" and "modernism," two terms whose meanings scholars have never stopped struggling to settle, but which could be summed up, simply, as follows. Where "modernity" signals a change in society's self-understanding, "modernism" names our artistic attempts to make sense of that change, and to forge new forms of expression that might, perhaps, prove adequate to it. On this line of thinking, "modernist" writers (like, say, Joyce) can be seen as working within the terms of a time which, as the sociologist Jürgen Habermas once said, refuses to "borrow criteria" from bygone eras, and sets out instead to reinvent them.

Robert Musil's *The Man Without Qualities* has taken a while to achieve recognition as a modernist masterpiece. This could be because it doesn't quite fit with such orderly models of what "the modern" might mean. The trouble is, Musil wasn't Joyce, nor Proust, and to weigh up his book as some Germanic answer to *Ulysses* or *À la Recherche du Temps Perdu* is to miss its point. Or rather, its lack of one. Because, however many times you read this famously unfinished novel, one thing's for sure: you'll never fully take the measure of its pointlessness.

Indeed, it'd be a stretch to say that this text even makes sense of itself, let alone of "modernity." Rather, its freewheeling narrative propels it somewhere beyond the familiar aims of modernist art. For unlike those others, this book doesn't want to build systems, to give order to memory or history, or to shore up anything much against its ruins. Instead, it lets those ruins remain as they are: incomplete, enigmatic, never entirely intelligible.

Born in 1880, Robert Musil lived quite a vacillating life. After abandoning a military career for one in engineering, he took a detour into doctoral work in psychology and philosophy. When offered an academic post he declined it, dropping out to devote himself solely to literature, poverty, and the pursuit of his interminable, impossible novel. We know he began work on *The Man Without Qualities* sometime in the 1920s, publishing its first two "volumes" in 1930 and 1932. Each went almost wholly unacknowledged, and indeed he grew to regret printing either, resenting the fixity they imposed on his ever-evolving work. Yet he went on writing nonetheless, and part of the project's third instalment was published after his death, in 1942. For a decade or so the novel was nearly forgotten, only resurfacing in the early 1950s, and first reaching English readers in 1953. The current translation by Sophie Wilkins and Burton Pike dates from 1995.

Experts have speculated at length on just how long the finished book might have been. The truth is that no one knows, not even Musil. By the end of its 1,130 pages, Wilkins and Pike's edition doesn't just fail to reach a conclusion; it barely even begins to begin. For many readers, myself included, this is the book's strangest, greatest achievement. What has to be grasped about *The Man Without Qualities* is that it's not just another "unfinished" masterpiece, in the sense that, say, Kafka's greatest books aren't finished. It's a *failed* masterpiece, and one whose failure ends up being the essence of its greatness. It's a failed book bound up with a failed life, in the way that many literary lives are failed. This point has been eloquently made by Maurice Blanchot, who says of Musil's book that it's

> an excessive work on which he labors for almost his entire creative life, a work that is for him the equivalent of his life. This book that he does not entirely master, that resists him and that he also resists, seeking to impose on it a plan that is perhaps not suitable for it. A strange experiment that makes his existence depend on a book.

An experiment, moreover, that's open-ended, and whose results get rerouted into its method. This idea of an endless, open process is what *The Man Without Qualities* is all about; it's central both to its composition and to what could be called, with some caution, its "plot."

The story is set in Vienna in 1913, and loosely concerns an attempt by the waning Austrian state to devise a "parallel campaign," an effort to ensure that the seventieth anniversary of Franz Joseph's reign eclipses Germany's celebration of thirty years under Wilhelm II. The campaign aims to capture what we might call the "hearts and minds" of the Austrian populace, but it's quickly shown up as an impossible plan. It didn't take place in historical time, of course, and nor does it ever occur in the time of the novel. The essence of the Empire will not be synthesized under the sign of a great idea. There will be no more great ideas, no unifying solutions. When Musil's protagonist, Ulrich, falls into the orbit of this endeavor, its endlessness only echoes his own indeterminacy; his failure to add up to anything more than the sum of the parts that he plays. For Ulrich, as for Austria, modern life's failure to fix its own meaning manifests as a mixture of crisis and promise. As the following famous description shows, this is precisely what Musil means when he says that Ulrich is a "man without qualities":

His appearance gives no clue to what his profession might be, and yet he doesn't look like a man without a profession either. He always knows what to do. He knows how to gaze into a woman's eyes. He can put his mind to any question at any time. He can box. He is gifted, strong-willed, open-minded, fearless, tenacious, dashing, circumspect – why quibble, suppose we grant him all those qualities – yet he has none of them! They have made him what he is, they have set his course for him, and yet they don't belong to him. When he is angry, something in him laughs. When he is sad, he is up to something. When something moves him, he turns against it. He'll always see a good side to every bad action. What he thinks of anything will always depend on some possible context – nothing is, to him, what it is: everything is subject to change, in flux, part of a whole, of an infinite number of wholes presumably adding up to a super-whole that, however, he knows nothing about.

For the literary critic Mark M. Freed, this acute concern for life's lived ambiguities – its contradictory traits, its impossible projects – is what makes *The Man Without Qualities* not so much a modernist novel as an "intervention in the philosophical discourse of modernity." Freed's definition of that discourse runs something like this. Modern life sets itself up through a series of exclusions and oppositions; it severs the self from the world, art from science, reason from feeling, and so on. Everything grows increasingly specialized, so that the more modern we get, the more we're caught up in an escalating state of alienation. Freed's remarkable study, *Robert Musil and the NonModern*, maps a terrain that's at odds with all this, using Musil to call into question some of our basic assumptions about what it means to be modern. In this account, Musil isn't so much a modernist (let alone a postmodernist) as someone who writes from both within and without, always "on the margins" of any such absolute categories. His is a literature of the "nonmodern," one which refuses to recognize modern conceptual boundaries. In short, *The Man Without Qualities* sets out to shake up all of the modern world's "purified distinctions." For an example of how this is played out, we need only consider the novel's opening passage:

A barometric low hung over the Atlantic. It moved eastward toward a high-pressure area over Russia without as yet showing any inclination to bypass this high in a northerly direction. The isotherms and isotheres were functioning as they should. The air temperature was appropriate relative to the annual mean temperature and to the aperiodic monthly fluctuations of the temperature. The rising and the setting of the sun, the moon, the phases of the moon, of Venus, of the rings of Saturn, and many other significant phenomena were all in accordance with the forecasts in the astronomical yearbooks. The water vapor in the air was at its maximal state of tension, while the humidity was minimal. In a word that characterizes the facts fairly accurately, even if it is a bit old-fashioned: It was a fine day in August 1913.

What makes this style of writing "nonmodern" is its method of merging the language of science with that of everyday life. In so doing, it fuses two of modernity's most deeply divided domains back together, not as opposites, but as equally valid alternatives, held in a state of suspension. Hence, neither way of describing the world is free or clear of the other, yet neither outdoes the other; neither takes precedent. As Freed rightly remarks, Musil's own name for this practice is "essayism" – a term whose meaning hinges on the etymological echoing of "essay" from *assay*, or "attempt." So, like the novel itself, like the life of its protagonist, and very much like the parallel campaign, an essay is only ever an attempt, never a means to an end. Indeed, it's only an essay so long as it escapes every ending, endlessly running away with itself. It's a goalless multiplication of options, and this, says Freed, is what makes it "neither modern nor postmodern." Instead, it's a new way of writing, thinking, and living that may just make possible "a nonmodern engagement with the problems of modernity."

In this vein, the real achievement of Freed's reading of Musil lies in his rich exposition of essayism as an "ethic," not just a literary technique but a view of the world, and a nonmodern means of moving through it. For Freed, Musil makes this explicit in his characterization of Ulrich as a man who attempts to *live essayistically*, taking the essay as "a model for the structure of experience," and remaking his life as an unending set of experiments. Here's Musil again, musing on Ulrich's own understanding of the events he encounters:

> It was more or less the way an essay itself explores a thing from many sides without wholly encompassing it... that he believed he could rightly survey and handle the world and his own life.

Picking up on this thought, Freed hones in on what must be Musil's most brilliant notion, and perhaps the prime example of a Musilian mixture of artistic statement and scientific discovery. Put simply, the idea behind Ulrich's "essayistic" lifestyle is that it's possible to live with an experimental *exactness*, steered by a "utopian idea of exact living." Like the best advances in both art and science, this bold new ethic is unnerving and unsentimental. If it brings on a feeling of vertigo, that's because it opens onto a dizzying well of potential that was formerly closed to us.

What's more, Freed goes on to show how Ulrich's ethic of essayism is enabled by the very thing that gives Musil's novel (or better yet, essay) its title: an absence of qualities. That is to say, Ulrich's role as a "man of possibility" turns out to *depend* on his being without qualities. As we saw above, the crux of his condition is that while he "has" qualities, he never quite "owns" them; they're independent of his essence. He's what we might call a well-rounded man, but one whose attributes can't quite account for any underlying substance. Thus, as Freed puts it, Ulrich is

> not a *what* that could possess qualities but a *how* in the sense of a being confronted with a range of possible ways of being... a mode of being poised to seize a wider range of possibilities of existence, not a substance to which qualities adhere.

If the actual forms a life takes in its time are arbitrary, a man without qualities is one who's aware of his arbitrariness, and whose life may then remain open to its own essayistic potential. An essayist doesn't experience things by accident; he *assays* them, tries them on for size, takes their measure. One troubling upshot of this, for Ulrich, is that he's even able to empathize with a character like Moosbrugger, the "sex murderer," whose pathological outlook has to be seen as a viable life among all lives, lived with its own internal coherence. That's what makes the essayist unsentimental; he's prepared to assay every option. It's also why Ulrich will finally try to transcend himself in an incestuous bond with his sister, Agathe. Such choices are logical outcomes of Musil's science of the soul, and of a personal essay that's always in search of new ways to outwit its end. Yet they're also procedures for preserving life's unfinished future. This is what Musil means when he hints that the unreached ending of every essay gives a glimpse of "utopia." To quote Blanchot again,

> the man without particularities is precisely the man of "not yet," the one who considers nothing as firm, stops every system, prevents every fixation, who does not say no to life, but not yet, who, finally, acts as if the world could never begin except on the next day.

Robert Musil and the NonModern is not without its flaws, first among which would be its unusually un-Musilian effort to provide an explanatory "theory" of Musil. Like Beckett, Musil is one of those writers whom critics should never take lightly. His work seems to tempt the critic into overzealous gestures, at the same time pre-empting precisely such gestures, containing them, and thereby escaping them. The problem with Freed's perspective lies in his eagerness to assume that philosophical frameworks can just be *applied* to Musil, and, for that matter, to literature. He makes a big deal of "homologies," and of what he calls "conceptual correspondences" relating Musil to Heidegger, Musil to Nietzsche, and so on. What risks getting lost in all this is a chance to let Musil speak for himself, or talk to himself: an application of Musil to Musil. After all, what is a "conceptual correspondence" anyway? And does it really give us a good way of thinking about fiction, or about thinking?

Perhaps this kind of criticism takes a bit too much for granted about its applications. The academic study of literature has reached a slightly strange understanding of itself, if it assumes that insights drawn from philosophy and social theory can straightforwardly account for aspects of fictional worlds, and fictional characters. In this sense, something odd gets glossed over in the midst of Freed's comparisons. Given that Ulrich famously advises one of his fellow characters that they should live "as if they were characters in a novel," what does it mean for a critic to come along and describe them as if they belonged to the same social world as himself? More work should surely be done to unearth these buried presuppositions. Until critics give some closer attention to *why* they're applying their theories to fictional objects, such applications might seem to rely on little more than a confusion of categories.

For all this, it's only fair to forgive Freed's book for falling prey to the most common problems of contemporary criticism. And of course, to ask for a critical study to be truly adequate to

Musil's art is to ask a great deal. *Robert Musil and the NonModern* offers the most exciting reading to date of Musil's experimental method, his essayism, and his uncompromising openness to the hope of a lived utopia. Yet after encountering such a commanding analysis, it's only right, if you love reading Musil, to want to pull his work out from under the weight of what's been applied to it. There's something about *The Man Without Qualities* that seems to resist conclusive criticism. Something not so much unfinished as uniquely continuous; infinite. The reason the novel is unlike anything else you'll ever read is because it goes on reading itself when you've finished reading it. Any kind of critical account would miss that mark, and how could a critic hope to catch up with a book that's always outrunning its readers? Musil's novel never will require to be read in order to exist. It will go on regardless, forever essaying itself, perfecting itself.

Reading Like a Loser

Malcolm Bull, *Anti-Nietzsche*

Sometimes it's said that we're all Nietzscheans now. Throughout critical and cultural theory, Nietzsche's ideas aren't so much studied as presupposed; they're part of the deep grammar of those fields, part of the furniture. These days, disquieting Nietzschean insights like, say, perspectivism (roughly, the doctrine that "there are no facts, only interpretations") have come to seem commonplace. At the same time, we've surely lost sight of what makes much of Nietzsche's thought politically unpalatable. Nietzsche is often repackaged as a "radical" thinker, by an academic establishment a little in love with its own naive notions of radicalism. Yet ideas aren't widely lauded as radical until they've already undergone a degree of diffusion, even dilution. In Nietzsche's case, the paradox plays out like this: we're only too eager to make "Nietzsche" a name that connotes "opposition," but as a result we fail to formulate any opposition to *him*. We celebrate Nietzsche for being anti-everything, but why is there no anti-Nietzsche?

Malcolm Bull's book aims to answer this question. To begin to do so, Bull argues, first we must ask why it hasn't been asked. What is it about Nietzsche's work that rules out resistance? How has his thought come to function as, in Bull's words, the "limit-philosophy" of our time? Bull makes the brilliant move of locating this "limiting" quality less in some abstract aspect of Nietzsche's thought than in the rhetoric of his writing. The problem is, in a sense, one of style. We all know how Hollywood movies induce us to "identify" with their heroic protagonists. Nietzsche's rhetorical strategy likewise invites us, as readers, to occupy a *position*; one that's utterly artificial, but that's made to appear irresistible. Consider, for instance, the well-known quote from *Ecce Homo*, "I am not a man, I am dynamite." Who, asks Bull, when reading these words, "has not felt the sudden thrill of something explosive within themselves?" Who hasn't appropriated some of that spirit, the energy that Nietzsche attributed only to himself? This is how we read when we read novels; in Nietzsche's case we make the mistake of adopting it as an approach to philosophy. Indeed, Nietzsche's philosophy is structurally similar to fiction, since it relies on eliciting the "right" response from its readers, by making that response its own rhetorical reward.

So, Nietzsche plays on our narcissism. His writing wants us, as Bull puts it, to "read for victory." Nietzsche always admired the Homeric "hero," set on a circular journey of self-discovery. Yet the reader is the real hero of Nietzsche's narratives, enticed into seeing him or herself as uniquely receptive to their radical arguments. We want to be just like Nietzsche, and Nietzsche knows this, which is why he encourages us to join him in enjoying fictional forms of strength, superiority, and self-expression. Faced with a choice between man and Superman, we naturally want to relate to the latter, even if Nietzsche's *Übermensch* is as unreal as any literary character. But if that's the case, how can readers resist the temptation to take Nietzsche's bait? As Bull rightly warns, rejecting Nietzsche is never easy. The problem is this: if Nietzsche's golden rule is "one must be victorious" (one must, like Nietzsche, *be* dynamite, be beyond good and evil) then surely to read Nietzsche critically would still be to read for victory, only this time over Nietzsche. That is, critique can't help but be circular; all our attempts to abandon Nietzsche simply bring us back to him.

Bull's solution, and the central claim of *Anti-Nietzsche*, consists of a startling statement: one can only sidestep Nietzsche's strategy by "reading him like a loser." Here Bull begins a sort of thought experiment, although it's far from an arid theoretical exercise. Instead, at times its tone approaches that of Swiftian satire. To read Nietzsche like a loser, Bull reasons, is not to reject his arguments but to accept them, even at their most reprehensible. If Nietzsche wants to write about rising above the herd, or enslaving the weak, then he's welcome to. Only, in following his flights of fancy, we're not to fall into the trap of identifying ourselves with his fictional victors. Rather, Bull says that we must "make ourselves the victims" of these texts. We should side with the slaves, the sick, the defeated, at all times turning Nietzsche's arguments against ourselves. In this way we can depart from Nietzsche "without having to meet him again," reading for victory neither with nor against him, but only ever against ourselves. In real life, after all, no one could hope to live up to Nietzsche's heroic ideal. In this sense, to read like a loser is to refuse to collude in a fiction of dominance. Reading Nietzsche will then make us feel like dirt, reminding us of our "weakness and mediocrity... our irremediable exclusion from the life that is possible only for those who are healthier, and more powerful."

For Bull, this self-defeating endeavor is more than a masochistic game; it's a fruitful starting point for a revolutionary "politics of failure." The idea here is to "justify and protect the herd of human failures." And not just the human ones, but all of those "lower" forms of life that stand to lose from Nietzsche's philosophy. Notably, in Nietzsche's system, Superman is to man as man is to ape. So if we want to undo Nietzsche's philosophy of superiority, why not make apes of ourselves? Opting out of Nietzsche's offer to make us more than human, we should strive instead to become something less. This is why Bull's book is swarming with animals. Sometimes it reads less like straight philosophy than creative *conte philosophique*; it's a fable full of dogs and rats and even, at one point, an "autonomous simian group" whom Bull suggests should be housed in the Louvre: "the long galleries could be used for sleeping and recreation, the Jardin des Tuileries for foraging."

But beneath such satirical speculations there's a serious aim.

For Bull, Nietzsche's hierarchical placement of species plays into his broader conservatism; his elitism; even his fascism. This is because his "social ecology" is meant to maximize value by restricting the range of entities entitled to enjoy it. Simply put, the substance of Nietzsche's account of animal life is that it is valueless; meaningless. For him, humans alone heroically make sense of the world, remaking its meaning in their own image. Bull shows how this line of thought feeds into later philosophies, like Heidegger's, where humanity is held aloft as the "shepherd of Being," and the driving force behind the fate of civilization. One only has to look at Heidegger's own political fate to see how this conceptual exclusion of the "subhuman" can have disastrous consequences. So, Bull's point is that a progressive politics will be one which refuses to segregate humans from animals. Against Nietzsche's claim that we ourselves are the source of all meaning, the best countermove we can make is to side with the subhuman, "extending the boundaries of society to let other species in." To do so is to see how politics can become "a species-changing practice."

What's more, to extend the limits of society is also to stretch those of culture. And for Bull, the cultural counterpart of the subhuman is that much misunderstood figure, the *philistine*. Here it's worth remembering that "receptivity to the aesthetic is the ticket to privilege in Nietzsche's world." From *The Birth of Tragedy* onwards, Nietzsche's attitude to art is elitist to say the least. In fact, for him the ability to create and appreciate art is the surest sign of social mastery. Nietzsche's elite must be, as George Santayana once put it, "cruelly but *beautifully* strong," where beauty and strength are essentially one and the same. If we're to live like losers, then, we really ought to get art wrong. By putting ourselves in the place of those who can't grasp the aesthetic, who clumsily fail to *evaluate* art, maybe we'll find a way out of Nietzsche's order of cultural value. Apes that we are, let's not be afraid to embarrass ourselves in front of the connoisseurs. The real revolutionary move is to claim a position not outside of culture, but *beneath* it. More boldly still, Bull insists that this "annihilation of art" mustn't merely pave the way for new aesthetic practices; instead, philistinism beckons us "beyond art altogether." It invites us to imagine a world after art – a future in which aesthetic appreciation has "disappeared," clearing our field of vision, and maybe, in so doing, disclosing "a new horizon."

Bull's book is full of such counterintuitive insights. In the end though, its brilliance lies less in its contrarian claims – its eloquent defenses of failure and philistinism – than its subtle tactic of tracking Nietzsche's arguments in ways that work against them. *Anti-Nietzsche* advocates an egalitarian practice of "levelling out;" a lowering of standards whose goal is to equalize everyone, including those "below the existing threshold." But Bull asks us to do more than just abandon our conceited sense of strength and beauty. His book remodels revolutionary politics, not as a Nietzschean act of revaluation, but as an experience of radical, runaway *entropy*. Of course, this corrosive force was already known to Nietzsche, whose own name for it was "nihilism." But Bull shows that where Nietzsche wrote of "overcoming" nihilism, his real investment was in arresting it. Nihilism is just a word for the way modern life propels us toward new forms of equalization; it's an entropic process which, once unleashed, can't be put back in the box. Seen in this light, Nietzsche's longing for inequality may really have been a last-ditch attempt to reterritorialize nihilism. Thus, *Anti-Nietzsche* pursues Nietzsche's logic, but pulls out all the stops. Nietzsche's mythical heroes stabilize society by exercising their individual wills; by positing values. What Bull does is call for us to fall short of such values, thereby removing the limits on entropy, and eventually coming together to become "less than we might otherwise be."

The World's Disappearance

Cathy Caruth, *Literature in the Ashes of History*

During the last couple of decades, debates in literary theory have lent the term "trauma" a scope which outstrips its standard psychiatric usage. In the influential field of "trauma studies," trauma functions as more than merely a diagnostic category – rather, it represents a collective concern. To quote the noted trauma scholar Shoshana Felman, trauma is now taken to embody "an essential dimension of human and historical experience, and a new type of understanding of historical causality and temporality." In fact, Felman goes so far as to declare that "the twentieth century can be defined as a century of trauma."

The rise of this "trauma paradigm" is partly attributable to the work of Cathy Caruth – author of the landmark study *Unclaimed Experience*, and now a new volume, *Literature in the Ashes of History*. Caruth's academic career, like Felman's, was forged at Yale in the 1980s, back when that university was the American nucleus of deconstruction. This environment directly inspired Caruth's writing on trauma, which remains recognizably deconstructive in its rhetorical moves. For instance, Caruth claims that trauma is intrinsically paradoxical, or "aporetic," to adopt the jargon. In both its clinical and its cultural aspects, trauma is a condition in which "the most direct seeing of a violent event may occur as an inability to know it," entailing that "its truth is bound up with its crisis of truth," and its accuracy is ensnared in error.

Caruth finds support for this line of thought in Freud's *Beyond the Pleasure Principle*. There, Freud posits that traumatic events aren't directly experienced the first time around. Instead, they intrude into consciousness only *belatedly*, in the form of flashbacks or repetitions. In this regard, trauma raises far-reaching questions about our ownership of our experiences. Following Freud, Caruth describes traumatic memories as inaccessible to introspection, meaning that they must remain "unclaimed." As she puts it, it is impossible to take "possession" of trauma, because "to be traumatized is precisely to be possessed." Furthermore, insofar as trauma is only identifiable after the fact (i.e. in the return of repressed experiences) it also complicates common conceptions of time. As Roger Luckhurst rightly observes, "no narrative of trauma can be told in a linear way: it has a time signature that fractures conventional causality."

So, trauma conveys a kind of *philosophical* force: it puts pressure on the epistemological status – and the evidential value – of recollected and recounted memories. Crucially though, for Caruth this pressure is not only epistemological; it is also necessarily ethical. As before, this is because trauma cuts across the personal and the historical. Indeed, Caruth contends that trauma is "not so much a symptom of the unconscious as a symptom of history," such that "the traumatized carry an impossible history within them." For her, it follows that this "impossible" quality must be *preserved* – particularly if we wish to bear "witness" to the histories that our traumas transmit. Once more, it is easy to see this idea's deconstructive colouring. Recalling Derrida's similar style of ethical thought, Caruth argues that trauma's aporia ought to be retained; that impossible histories call for appropriately unresolved types of testimony. In short, if we are ever to take stock of trauma, we must remain faithful to its "affront to understanding."

Caruth's new book begins by condensing these lines of inquiry into two questions: firstly, "what does it mean for history to disappear?" and then, by extension, "what does it mean to *speak* of a disappearing history?" The first question reflects Caruth's reading of twentieth-century history as itself traumatic – that is, as subject to the same sort of epistemological uncertainty, or "erasure," that structures traumatic experience. The second question expresses the ethical upshot of this idea: if history has become inaccessible, what kind of communicative act could do it justice? Throughout *Literature in the Ashes of History*, Caruth brings the first question into focus using the theories of Freud, Derrida, and Arendt. As the title suggests, the second question leads her to emphasize literary works – notably Balzac's novella *Le Colonel Chabert* and Ariel Dorfman's play *Death and the Maiden*.

To appreciate the importance that Caruth assigns to these literary texts, we must first understand the scale of her claim about history's "disappearance." At its most ambitious, this argument attempts to define nothing less than the nature of modern historical time. Caruth encapsulates that definition as follows:

The historicity of the twentieth, and now twenty-first, centuries... is not, as one might traditionally expect, constituted by events that create their own remembrance, but by events that destroy their own remembrance.

How exactly does an event destroy its remembrance? Caruth's descriptions of this issue share some of Derrida's weakness for wordplay; at times, her arguments circle rather superfluously around the meanings of terms like "touch," or the titular "ashes." However, a more precise sense of her intent can be gleaned from her readings of Arendt's late essays, "Truth and Politics" and "Lying in Politics." Tracking Arendt's analysis of twentieth-century political discourse (particularly in the context of totalitarian states, but also in terms of American policymaking during the Vietnam War) Caruth comments that "the public realm is not only the place that creates history, but also, and centrally, the place of the political lie that denies it." Essentially, modern political rhetoric tends to register "facts" only via the larger lies that foreclose them. For Arendt, this results in a perverse sort of reversal, whereby politics no longer "produces" lies, but is itself produced by them, such that it "works within" them. Ultimately then, the "political lie" serves less to repress reality than to replace it altogether. In this sense, history seems to come into being by means of its ongoing destruction.

If we live in a world which, as per Arendt, "erases memory in the very act of creating new events," how can our culture bear witness to that world's disappearance? Caruth's response to this problem relies on the distinctive resources of literature. The plots of her principal texts, by Balzac and Dorfman, each take place in the wake of a different historical trauma. Balzac's protagonist, a former French cavalry officer, is wounded in the Napoleonic Wars, and then accidentally declared dead. Returning to Paris, he later enters a legal battle with his remarried wife, from whom he attempts to reclaim not only his liquidated property, but, in a sense, his very identity. *Death and the Maiden* deals with a comparable recovery, only this time in the context of a former dictatorship (which Dorfman's stage directions describe as "probably Chile"). The play describes the plight of Paulina Salas, a survivor of political imprisonment, who tries to overcome her trauma by staging a disturbing "trial." The defendant, a stranger, may or may not be her former captor.

Basically, in both Balzac and Dorfman, what is at stake is the rebuilding of post-traumatic identity. In particular, these texts suggest how narratives of personal recovery can intersect with broader stories of historical transformation (whether that of the Bourbon Restoration, or of post-Pinochet Chile). Crucially though, Caruth's ethical take on trauma requires such stories to *resist* any overly easy resolution. As she argues in *Unclaimed Experience*, the value of literature as a vehicle for traumatic "testimony" lies precisely in its ability to accommodate ambiguity; in the way that fictional narratives waver between "knowing and not knowing." For this reason, her readings proceed in a characteristically deconstructive fashion. In searching these works for adequate ways of "witnessing" trauma – indeed, for "new modes of conceptual and historical survival" – she is effectively testing their inner fidelity to the "impossible."

The clearest example of what Caruth seems to mean by "survival" occurs in *Le Colonel Chabert* – specifically in its final few scenes, where Chabert opts out of reclaiming his title. Actually, a little like Melville's Bartleby, he opts out of pretty much everything; the last time we encounter him, he is living in an almshouse. As Caruth admits, "this hardly makes for a happy ending." However, where other critics have read these scenes "simply as a confirmation of Chabert's failure to attain his identity," Caruth discerns a subtle silver lining. For her, it is through Chabert's final "renunciation" that "the story opens the possibility for him to name himself anew." In other words, by relinquishing his repeated attempts to "possess" his experience, Balzac's protagonist transforms his trauma into a new form of life. In the end, he attains "a peculiar capacity to name, precisely, his very survival in the form of an ultimate loss."

Whether we are completely convinced by this claim depends, perhaps, on the store we set by the standard tropes of Caruth's particular critical school. It's not uncommon, in this genre of theoretical criticism, for the sweeping declaration (history itself is traumatic) and the ensuing ethical demand (all testimonies must be uncertain) to leave little real room for maneuver. (In this respect, Caruth's reading of Balzac rather resembles Gilles Deleuze's dubious account of the deathbed scene in *Our Mutual Friend* as an image of liberation from worldly identity.) When literary works are required to bear such an overpowering weight, perhaps it is unsurprising that they deliver only the slenderest measures of freedom. As Mark McGurl has remarked in a different context, many critics would do well to make more of a "conceptual allowance for the potential *triviality* of the literary work as a historical force." Admittedly, casting Caruth in this light might be a little too critical; her book should indeed be commended for trying to capture trauma's transformation into an "imperative to live." However, the question it leaves unsatisfactorily answered is whether literature, or theory, can finally furnish sufficient foundations for that imperative.

Steep Turns, Surprising Vistas

D.N. Rodowick, *Elegy for Theory*

What's left to be said about "theory?" The theory wars of the 1970s and 80s have long since lost their fervor. Gone are the glory days – or, some might say, the ice age – when theory was thrust to the forefront of critical consciousness. Today, theory isn't exactly espoused or opposed so much as unthinkingly presupposed – if not simply shrugged off as passé. In this sense, theory has slipped into a state of semi-invisibility. Many of the most pioneering insights of "high theory" are now so institutionalized that they're less readily recognizable *as* theory; ideas once regarded as revolutionary have been incorporated into the routine practices of academic disciplines. At the same time, such disciplines seem increasingly keen to deny theory's lasting effects; thus, theory is rather ritualistically declared "dead," and we assume that we're safely "after theory."

But if theory really is a thing of the past, its status as such could open it up for retrospective reconsideration. Insofar as a certain era or genre of theory feels like it's "over," perhaps its historical closure leaves it newly illuminated, in ways which weren't possible when it was pressingly present. For this reason, a new strand of scholarship appears to be emerging: one which treats theory less as an instrument than an object of study in its own right. François Cusset led the way with *French Theory*, a contextual account of the impact of Derrida, Deleuze, and co on American academia. More recently, Mark Currie has historicized the "invention of deconstruction," while Judith Ryan has illustrated the influence of literary theory on postwar fiction. For these authors and others, theory, it seems, is still on the table – only now it's seen from a shifted, reflexive perspective.

D.N. Rodowick's *Elegy for Theory* echoes this trend, and also

extends it. Rodowick's field of expertise is film studies – a discipline which he helped develop (he founded Yale's film studies
major in 1985, and recently directed the PhD program at
Harvard) and which, throughout his career, he has surveyed
with a keenly historical sensibility (a previous book, *The Crisis of
Political Modernism*, offered an authoritative account of the
heyday of film theory from 1968 through the 1980s). In some
respects, *Elegy for Theory* reads like a sequel to that earlier work,
although its scope is much more ambitious. While remaining
rooted in the intellectual history of cinema studies, here
Rodowick situates that history within a longer, larger story.
Significantly, he seeks to show how theory's changing applications to film exemplify its more general trajectory across the arts
and humanities – a narrative whose sheer scale and complexity,
he contends, now need to be brought into focus:

> Embedded within the concept of theory is a discontinuous
> history of conceptual usage as long as it is incomplete. Each
> time we evoke or invoke theory in the humanities, we lift the
> weight of this history on our backs, or more likely, we tread
> lightly upon it, as if to leave undisturbed the bones of our
> ancestors, unaware of how many geological layers lie beneath
> our feet.

Refreshingly then, Rodowick wishes to excavate the fossil record
of theory, rather than adding another two cents to the increasingly tired arguments "for" or "against" it. Stepping back from
such controversies, he stresses instead the more modest but
important point that "theory has a history" – a history which the
rhetorical fireworks of the theory wars have too often obscured.
Regardless of whether we wish to preserve theory or resist it,
"our picture of theory," Rodowick argues, "has become cloudy
and unfocused, because we have forgotten its history, or become
blinded to it." Therefore, the aim of this "elegy" is to restore

some much-needed precision to the way we conceive of theory as such: Rodowick is concerned not with contestation, but with conceptual clarification.

Indeed, if theory has recently been controversial, Rodowick makes us aware that it was always thus. Theory, he claims, is an inherently "unstable" concept, conditioned by a "history of unruliness" which "reaches back 2,500 years." Accordingly, *Elegy for Theory* tracks several centuries' worth of seismic shifts in the concept's semantics, ranging from classical Greek accounts of *theoria* (a term whose etymological echo of "theater" already foreshadows the link between theory and film) to eighteenth-century German aesthetics, before finally reaching the more familiar terrain of "French" theory post-'68. The resulting picture resembles a kind of intellectual pinball game, in which the over-determined term "theory" (trailing various precursors and place-holders) bounces from Aristotle to Althusser and beyond, sometimes colliding with well-known names (Hegel, Kristeva) and sometimes with figures specific to cinema studies (Canudo, Aristarco). As Rodowick acknowledges, the effect can often seem somewhat chaotic:

> My attempts to understand the conceptual vicissitudes of theory have veered wildly in perspective, sometimes plunging into one or two texts in florid detail, making them carry the weight of an entire discursive formation in the space of a few pages, then retreating to the horizon to frame the most panoramic view possible.

Crucially though, this approach produces precisely the kind of "conceptual clarity" Rodowick seeks. That is, in the case of an "unruly" concept like theory, clarification should not be confused with simplification. Rather, the method of historical recon-struction must reflect the unruliness of its object. In this regard, Rodowick follows Michel Foucault in preferring the detours of "genealogy" to the disingenuous neatness of linear history. Foucault famously defined genealogy as a kind of historical investigation that deliberately "disturbs what was previously considered immobile," "fragments what was thought unified," and "shows the heterogeneity of what was imagined consistent with itself." Similarly, Rodowick sets out to render theory in all its self-inconsistency, not as a spurious whole (the mirage we conjure when we converse casually about "theory") but as a fractured palimpsest, fissured by historical fault-lines – an almost ungraspably complex object, which "retreats from us as rapidly as we approach it." Consequently, "a genealogy of theory cannot confuse clarity with the search for origins." Straying from any predictably straightforward path, Rodowick maps theory's multiple "culs-de-sac, secret passages, steep turns, and surprising vistas," the better to disclose "not one identity, but many lines of descent."

Two such lines tend to recur throughout Rodowick's labyrinthine account, combining and recombining in constant tension and entanglement. One of these threads connects theory to philosophy, through an "aesthetic discourse" shaped by the long shadow of Hegel. The other ties it to the rise of modern science, via various flavors of positivism and empiricism. In this sense, theory seems to "hover in an unstable space, as if held unsteadily" between twin poles or attractors. Rodowick shows how the push and pull of these forces has formed theory as we know it today. In the postwar period, for instance, aesthetic conceptions of theory give way to what Rodowick calls the "discourse of signification" – a "desire for formalization" which peaks in the structuralist project of systematizing the human sciences. Rodowick's genealogy of structuralism takes in some intriguing twists and turns, traveling back through the French "filmology" movement to Russian formalism, and further. Yet these are not to be seen as steps in a causal progression; instead, they represent nodes in a network, "capillaries" branching out from "the beating heart of positivism." Later the pendulum swings back again, when Derrida and the post-structuralists disrupt the "epistemological confidence" of their predecessors. But beneath these differing configurations, an underlying rhythm remains: theory is formed, deformed, and reformed in the shifting space between science and philosophy.

Rodowick's most detailed description of the formation of a theoretical discourse – that is, of the way in which a specific iteration of "theory" arises to organize this fluid space – occurs late in the book, in a section focused on the French film theorist Christian Metz. Rodowick credits Metz with the "invention" of modern film theory – and, through a close reading of this critic's early essay "Le cinéma: Langue ou Langage," he articulates how such inventions come about. One of the most striking traits of Metz's essay is its performative search for precursors to the type of theory – here, a systematic "film semiology" – that it seeks to construct. In other words, Metz formulates his theory by reflecting on his forerunners (principally, assorted proponents of the "aesthetic discourse") and, in so doing, sweeping them up into the newly-minted discourse of signification. As Rodowick explains, Metz's essay not only surveys the history of writing on film, but retrospectively rewrites it, such that "theory enters the ordinary language of academic discourse as if it had always been there," as if earlier authors like Canudo "were and always had been theorists." Through his assemblage of a set of precedents for theory, Metz therefore "reformats the aesthetic discourse in the structure of the discourse of signification."

But beyond the immediate impact of this intervention, Metz's essay might be of still deeper significance. Rodowick goes on to suggest that Metz, in making this methodological move, "was one of the first key figures to adopt a *metatheoretical* perspective in film study, constructing theory as an object, examining its history, and testing its present and potential claims to generate knowledge." And this strongly recursive, self-reflexive standpoint – which Rodowick dubs "the metatheoretical attitude" – is arguably the driving dynamic of theory "as we have lived and still live it." Perhaps it could even be said that theory creates and renews itself precisely by thus folding back on its previous forms, so as to "project new epistemological spaces," redefining its history and thereby redrawing its future horizons. This, to my mind, is the most important insight of Rodowick's book. As he puts it,

> Every historical moment of theoretical awakening is, as it were, to some degree metacritical or metatheoretical. In key moments of discursive ramification or reformulation, an idea of theory suddenly becomes conscious of itself and its apparent history. [These are] moments of rupture, reconsideration, and retrojection in which theory takes itself as its own object; examines and reconfigures its genealogy, conceptual structure, and terminology, and posits for itself a new identity and cultural standing.

Moreover, if theory moves forward by looking back, then Rodowick's own work epitomizes the metacritical spirit it describes. In this essential respect, *Elegy for Theory* surpasses its humbly stated aim of "clarifying" the history of a concept. While it is true that readers of Rodowick's book will discover new insights into the story of theory, the exhilaration aroused by those "steep turns and surprising vistas" stems as much from the structure and form of the story's telling: to follow Rodowick's argument is, in a way, to witness the spiraling swerve of theory enveloping and comprehending itself. It remains to be seen where Rodowick's next book will lead – he hints that it will relinquish high theory in favor of a new conception of philosophy. And yet his elegy's very existence suggests, somehow, that whatever animates theory is alive and well. Toward the end of this book, Rodowick writes of the era of theory that "to feel one's self at the end of something inspires reflection on its ends." In itself, his inspired reflection revives the stream of ideas on which it reflects; if this is only an elegy, it's one that instils its object with endless energy.

Acknowledgments

The pieces collected in this book originally appeared in a range of online and print publications, between 2011 and 2014. Those publications include, among others, the *Los Angeles Review of Books*, the *Times Literary Supplement*, *Radical Philosophy*, *The New Inquiry*, *The Rumpus*, *Electric Literature*, *PN Review*, *The Quarterly Conversation*, *Review 31*, *Music & Literature*, *3:AM Magazine*, *Berfrois*, *Full Stop*, and *Open Letters Monthly*. I would like to thank the various editors I've worked with during these years, whether on one piece or several – including Scott Esposito, Darcy Cosper, Arne de Boever, Michael Caines, David Cunningham, Sam Sacks, Benjamin Samuel, Jesse Miller, Jeffrey Zuckerman, and too many others to mention. I'm particularly grateful to Andrew Gallix for publishing my first ever book review, and for making me a co-editor at *3:AM* shortly afterwards. I also want to thank Tariq Goddard and everyone at Zero, for giving me the opportunity to gather my writing together. The artist Betsy Birkey kindly provided a beautiful image for my front cover. This book is dedicated to Branwen Pugh (1989–2009), a companion through many years of reading.

zero
books

Contemporary culture has eliminated both the concept of the public and the figure of the intellectual. Former public spaces – both physical and cultural – are now either derelict or colonized by advertising. A cretinous anti-intellectualism presides, cheerled by expensively educated hacks in the pay of multinational corporations who reassure their bored readers that there is no need to rouse themselves from their interpassive stupor. The informal censorship internalized and propagated by the cultural workers of late capitalism generates a banal conformity that the propaganda chiefs of Stalinism could only ever have dreamt of imposing. Zer0 Books knows that another kind of discourse – intellectual without being academic, popular without being populist – is not only possible: it is already flourishing, in the regions beyond the striplit malls of so-called mass media and the neurotically bureaucratic halls of the academy. Zer0 is committed to the idea of publishing as a making public of the intellectual. It is convinced that in the unthinking, blandly consensual culture in which we live, critical and engaged theoretical reflection is more important than ever before.